Praise for Lobster Rolls & Blueberry Pie

"Rebecca Charles's food at Pearl Oyster Bar sings the clear song of joy and gustatory delight at the operatic level of La Scala. Her recipes are simple, direct, and almost as easy as eating at my favorite lunch spot on the planet—just down Cornelia Street."

—MARIO BATALI, *chef-owner, Babbo, Lupa, Esca, and Otto*

"A charming memoir of summers spent on the coast of Maine."

—*Daily News*

"Personal and evocative."

—*San Francisco Examiner*

"A satisfying mix of memoir and cookbook."

—*Boston Globe*

"A charming, well-written account of three generations of women and their summer adventures in Kennebunkport."

—*Portland Phoenix*

"A book bound to leave readers feeling that summer just can't come soon enough."

—*Los Angeles Times*

"Charles follows three generations of women in her family on their summer retreats to Kennebunkport, Maine, wrapping her narrative in recipes and culinary reminiscences."

—*Elle*

"If Chef Rebecca Charles's, with Deborah DiClementi, sunny tales of her family vacations in Maine don't jostle your own memories, the mouthwatering title recipe and 70 others she includes, will."

—*Marie Claire*

"A homespun travelogue that's breezy, practical and likely to charm even armchair gourmands not partial to the beach."

—Baltimore Sun

"You can while away the wait reading chef Rebecca Charles's wonderful new book. . . . Part memoir, part culinary reminiscence, and, of course, part cookbook, *Lobster Rolls* is especially a tribute to Charles's grandmother . . . and to Maine."

—New York magazine

"I remember Rebecca's grandmother, Pearle, who was in the chorus when I sang at New York City Opera. She made the best shortbread cookies, and Rebecca's book is just as delicious as those cookies!"

—Beverly Sills

Lobster Rolls & Blueberry Pie

THREE GENERATIONS OF RECIPES AND STORIES FROM SUMMERS ON THE COAST OF MAINE

REBECCA CHARLES OF PEARL OYSTER BAR AND DEBORAH DICLEMENTI

WM

WILLIAM MORROW
An Imprint of HarperCollinsPublishers

FIRST HARPER PAPERBACK EDITION PUBLISHED 2006.

FIRST WILLIAM MORROW PAPERBACK EDITION PUBLISHED 2016.

Designed by Kelly Hitt

Oyster, fish, and lobster illustrations by Maria Nazzoli.

Photographs on pages vi–vii, 36, 61, 107, 123, 148, 154–55, 159, 166, 177, 179, 189, 198, and 204, and in color insert, by Michael Donnelly. Photograph on page 220 courtesy of the Seaside Motor Lodge.

The Library of Congress has catalogued the hardcover edition as follows:

Library of Congress Cataloging-in-Publication Data
Charles, Rebecca.
Lobster rolls & blueberry pie : three generations of recipes and stories
from summers on the coast of Maine / Rebecca Charles and Deborah DiClementi.– 1st ed.
p. cm.
ISBN 978-0-06-051583-6
1. Cookery, American—New England style. 2. Goldsmith family.
I. Title: Lobster rolls and blueberry pie. II. DiClementi, Deborah. III. Title.
TX715.2.N48C42 2003
641.5974-dc21
2003041341

ISBN 978-0-06-051583-6 (pbk.)

16 17 18 SCP 10 9 8 7 6 5 4 3

For my mother,

Eleanor,

and her mother,

Pearle

CONTENTS

All art is autobiographical.

The pearl is the oyster's autobiography.

~ Federico Fellini

Foreword

If you had to make up a fairy tale that might explain Pearl, Rebecca Charles's remarkable little restaurant in Greenwich Village, I think you'd start with a genie who also happened to be a venture capitalist. Encountering the genie through circumstances we needn't go into, Rebecca reveals her dream of opening a restaurant that strips away everything that's extraneous and maybe even deleterious to enjoying terrific food in pleasant surroundings—no gaggle of assistants in the kitchen to dilute what can be controlled by the chef, no expensive table settings and giant flower arrangements soaking up money that could be used for ingredients, no maître d' who might turn snotty if he's been rejected for yet another part off-Broadway.

"Go to it," the genie says, and hands her the keys to a tiny storefront on Cornelia Street, just a couple of blocks from my house. (Whoever makes up the fairy tale gets to control the location.)

When the genie drops by, just before opening night, to look over the restaurant Rebecca's designed, he says, "But there are no tables!"

"Extraneous," says Rebecca, who is too busy shucking oysters to go into long explanations. "The counter's fine."

"But my mother's coming to the opening," says the genie. "She's not a counter sort of person."

So Rebecca puts in one table. She's not against compromise, except when it comes to the quality of the food.

As it happens, I disagree with the genie's mom. I love sitting at the counter at Pearl, tucking away salt-encrusted shrimp or a lobster roll or whichever fish Rebecca considered fresh enough to grill that day. The counter crowd is always friendly. If you manage to look sufficiently interested, the person at the next seat might offer you a steamer and the person next to him might explain to you, in a kindly way, that you made a terrible mistake not ordering the clam chowder. It isn't difficult to figure out the source of their good humor: The food is making them happy.

I was naturally pleased when Rebecca told me that Pearl was planning to expand into the space next door, providing room for enough tables to delight the genie's mother and her friends. But I think it will take me a while to use the tables regularly. The counter's fine.

~ Calvin Trillin

INTRODUCTION

THERE IS SOMETHING VERY SPECIAL ABOUT SUMMER VACATION. To me, it means one thing: the historic Maine town I have been visiting since I was a baby. After hundreds of sweltering hours behind the stove at my New York City restaurant Pearl Oyster Bar, I finally get my reward at the end of August, when I close Pearl for two weeks and drive north to Kennebunkport, Maine. My family has been making the same trip since 1919, which is why every time I go back to visit, it feels like going home.

My first trip to Gooch's Beach when I was seven months old.

From the small bridge that spans Gooch's Creek, I watch three peach- and teal-colored rowboats tethered to one another, their mirror images undulating in the water. Next to the road, the gold, purple, and pink spires of lupine, a flower of imperial height that grows wild throughout Maine, follow me on my morning walks. Lobstermen's cottages dotted around the harbor appear through fogs thick with salt—gingerbread houses trimmed in bright colors and wrapped with strings of buoys, like huge crayons, lobster pots stacked in the yard. I am the third generation in my family to summer in Kennebunkport, where, just like me, my family went to escape the noise and heat of New York City. Coming from a family of scant traditions, for me the Kennebunks are more than just an escape—they are a part of my history and my future.

Not too long ago I found a photo of me on my first trip to Kennebunkport. There is a tuft of hair on my otherwise bald seven-month-old head, and my chubby arms and legs are outstretched. I'm wearing nothing but a poofy pair of pants over my diaper and an enormous smile on my face. Even without the striped beach towel spread over the sand beneath me, I would

A pile of Goldsmiths on the Beach. From left, Aunt Jenny, Goldie, Ted, Pearle, Ellie, Aunt Minna, and Marc.

know just by that smile that I was on Gooch's Beach. As children, my mom, my brother, and I and two generations of cousins all enjoyed rustic Maine summers filled with adventure. We explored stretches of beach, throwing ourselves into punishing waves. Rocky coves protected us kids from the heavier tides and offered tidal pools filled with small red and blue crabs, mussels, and every now and then, a tiny baby lobster.

Years later when I opened Pearl Oyster Bar, it was those Kennebunkport summers, as well as the decade I spent living there, that gave me the idea for a Maine-inspired seafood restaurant. My family, especially my grandmother Pearle, after whom I named the restaurant, was also an inspiration, and when I decided to write a cookbook I knew it would have to be more than a collection of recipes: It was about family history too. How, for instance, did my young, liberal, cosmopolitan Jewish family end up visiting a conservative, seafaring town like Kennebunkport way back in 1919? Since I never really knew that much about the Goldsmiths, it was going to be a challenge. I grew up in a family who didn't talk about themselves. As my cousin Louise says, "Goldsmiths never talk about Goldsmiths." Not that this was unusual for a generation who lived most of their lives before the 1970s, when the parsing and dissecting of feelings became a national pastime.

So I ransacked the withering old Victorian in Kennebunkport, Maine, that my mom had purchased as a summer house years ago. Because of our busy lives, however, it had become a rental property and storage space for my grandparents' trunks. There were sepia-toned photographs, packets of letters, and stacks of old postcards that hadn't been looked at in decades. I asked questions of everyone who was still alive (in the family and out of it), read old obituaries from newspapers across the country, and tried to track down long lost family members on the Internet. Slowly my grandparents and Goldsmiths of all ages began to reveal themselves. What became startlingly clear to me was that without my family, the majority of whom I had never met, there would have been no Pearl Oyster Bar.

Collectively and separately my family all fell in love with Maine, especially the three generations of Goldsmith women, Pearle, my mother Eleanor, and me. The summer days we spent together are always with me: the picnics on Gooch's Beach, cocktails on the breakwater surrounded by the Atlantic Ocean, and visits to roadside vegetable stands for tiny Maine blueberries, juicy ears of sweet corn, and plump tomatoes so fresh they're still speckled with mud. Each year I return to eat lobsters at Nunan's and chicken potpie at the Maine Diner. I walk the same beaches, the same wide expanse of sand I did as a child, smiling the same smile, just as I did last summer, the summer before, and almost every summer of my life.

PART ONE

KENNEBUNKPORT BOUND

GOLF LINKS, KENNEBUNKPORT, ME.

It Happened One Night

BY ALL ACCOUNTS, MY GREAT UNCLE, SAM GOLDSMITH, THE
BROTHER OF MY GRANDFATHER SOLOMON, HAD A GREAT APPETITE,
NOT JUST FOR FOOD LIKE EVERY-
ONE ELSE IN MY FAMILY, BUT FOR
LIFE IN GENERAL. He sought
adventure the way others seek money
or romance, traveled extensively
exploring new places, and made a
point of living well. A dapper barrel-
chested man, handsome with thick
black hair and the Goldsmith smile,
my Uncle Sam was partial to white
ducks in summer, black and white
wing tips, snappy ties, expensive blaz-
ers, and always a good cigar. By 1919
he had married his wife Jenny and
they had become parents to a daughter, Gertrude. Over the next few years,
two sons, Marc and Ted, would follow.
Having children didn't slow Uncle
Sam down, he just put the kids in the
car and brought them along.

Sol and Sam were alike in many
ways. The brothers Goldsmith

Uncle Sam, circa 1933,
in front of a stone wall
across from the Forest
Hill House, the family's
favorite spot for
portraits.

shared a wicked sense of humor, but where my grandfather Sol, affec-
tionately known to all as "Goldie," had a warmer, more gentle charm, Sam
was the showman, a trait that made him seem a bit like P. T. Barnum as he
entered middle age. But it was Uncle Sam's search for adventure and con-

Uncle Sam on the beach.

stant attempts to broaden his world that brought my family to Kennebunkport.

During the summer of 1918, he loaded up his Model T and drove with Jenny all the way up the Eastern Seaboard from Brooklyn, New York, into Canada and on up to Nova Scotia. They made the two thousand-mile-plus round-trip over the course of several weeks and each evening as the sun dipped below the horizon, Sam would begin keeping a sharp eye out for some quaint New England town to visit for the night. Family lore has it that it was while on their way back to Brooklyn one night, when Uncle Sam and Aunt Jenny were completely exhausted and ready to fall asleep at the wheel, that they happened upon Kennebunkport, a Yankee Brigadoon rising out of the sea mist.

Uncle Sam immediately liked the town and not only did they add a couple of days onto their trip to explore the area, they also decided to come back the next year for their entire vacation. How could Uncle Sam and Aunt Jenny not have been charmed by this part of Maine's southern coast? A small resort town, Kennebunkport is part of a larger area that locals, for brevity's sake, have nicknamed the Kennebunks. Strung in a loose line along a postcard-perfect stretch of Maine coastline just below Portland, the Kennebunks also include the town of Kennebunk, with its old sea captains' mansions, wood and stone reminders of a lost romantic era, and the beautiful Kennebunk Beach; the low-key summer community of Goose Rocks, two golden crescents of sand banked by dunes; and the tiny, hardworking fishing port of Cape Porpoise, with a round harbor filled with boats like a child's bathtub.

Sam and Jenny were used to the cement corridors of Brooklyn and Manhattan, and so they loved being out of doors. New York may have offered the Goldsmiths cultural advantages, but in Kennebunk they could sail on the Atlantic, fish in the Kennebunk River, or walk the salt marshes, spotting birds and other wildlife. But the Kennebunks displayed a mere microcosm of Maine's natural gifts. Magic had swept across the state ten thousand years before, when Ice Age glacial plates scraped the land, leaving behind eskers, deep rivers, even a fjord. They created hundreds of exquisite islands, now the chic destinations for well-to-do vacationers and summer residents.

Before Uncle Sam left the Kennebunks he made plans to return the very next summer and hoped to entice his brother and wife, my grandparents, to come along too. Pearle and Goldie didn't come that next summer, though. Perhaps they needed more convincing, or maybe it was money. As always, Sam forged ahead anyway. In late July of 1919, Sam drove up to the Kennebunks with Jenny and the newest addition to the family, their infant daughter Gertrude, and didn't return until after Labor Day.

Brooklyn, 1919

AUGUST 1919 TURNED OUT TO BE A MONTH OF SIZZLING, TAR-BLISTERING HEAT, AND WITH BRICK AND MORTAR ON ALL SIDES THE CITY WAS LIKE A GIANT KILN, BAKING ITS RESIDENTS UNTIL THEY WERE BRITTLE. For six weeks my Uncle Sam and Aunt Jenny flooded my grandparents' mail slot at 129 Patchin Avenue in Brooklyn with a flurry of postcards from Kennebunkport. The cards depicted happy beach scenes with cottages by the sea and cool pine trees. As my grandparents sat at the small kitchen table plucking them from the rest of the mail, the smell of kasha and cabbage wafting up from nearby apartments, just looking at these cards must have provided relief from the soot and noise of the city in summer.

A flurry of postcards from Uncle Sam and Aunt Jenny dated 1919.

The three-hundred-mile trip to the Kennebunks is a 5½-hour car ride now, but in 1919 driving from Brooklyn was a substantial trip, especially when it was made on dirt roads in very early cars with thin, ropy tires, and horsehair-stuffed seats, years before shock absorbers were invented. But Uncle Sam loved a good drive, and long after he had moved his family out to Chicago years later, he continued to return to Maine most summers. Even as he grew old (and he lived to be ninety-four), he made many of those trips in the car.

Aunt Jenny wrote most of the postcards, and every available space was taken up with the carefree, joyous sentiments of vacationers with little else to do but indulge themselves. For Aunt Jenny that meant sitting on the hotel's side lawn, a pine-scented haven, and rocking baby Gertrude. Uncle Sam swam in the icy Atlantic and was forever in pursuit of the perfect chowder. In my experience, this is a challenging pursuit. A great chowder is a study in balance, from the thickness to the play between the clams and salt pork to the almost underuse of potato. In those days, good chowder meant cream fresh from local farms and clams just out of the water.

Content and wanting to share this experience with his brother, Sam contrived to plant the seeds of Maine summers in my grandparents' heads in at least one postcard: *You must come up here dear brother and bring little Beck. The beach is lovely but the food, ahhh! Love, Sam.* It must have done the trick because those postcards, a handful of one-cent souvenirs, ended up determining my grandparents' vacation plans for the next fifty or so summers. They would also play a part in my own history nearly eighty years later when I opened Pearl Oyster Bar and inadvertently put the humble little lobster roll on dozens of Manhattan menus—but I'm getting ahead of myself.

A Resort Is Born

Pearle had also been away that summer, to Atlantic City, where she was recuperating from some mysterious early-century ailment that was unspecified but serious enough to put her in the hospital for a while. The steel piers and hurdy-gurdy atmosphere of the boardwalk, however, could compare neither with the beautiful Maine seascapes or the stories of caches of shellfish being offered by local restaurants. Stories of good food alone were enough to entice my family to travel. So upon her return, Pearle and Goldie began making plans to go to Kennebunkport the very next summer. Places like Atlantic City were vacation spots, but Kennebunk Beach was a resort, a carefully planned one.

Through the early 1600s, only the Wabanakis roamed southern Maine, hunting and fishing. Nicknamed People of the Dawn, this local group of Native Americans included the Micmac, Passamaquoddie, Maliseet, and Penobscot tribes. The name Kennebunk is in fact from an ancient Native American word, *kinibanek,* that roughly means "long cut bank." It was a short trip from hunting and fishing ground to tourism opportunity. Only about 250 years passed between Maine's first European settlement and the creation of Kennebunk Beach, a real-life game of Monopoly, as a playground for the wealthy.

Kennebunk Beach was actually the contrivance of a band of wealthy Boston and Kennebunkport businessmen who incorporated into the Boston and Kennebunkport Seashore Company in 1872. The group wanted a chunk of desirable coastal land on which to build an exclusive resort community for upper-middle-class Boston families looking to escape the city each summer. Kennebunk Beach was a natural for their plan, since it combined a close proximity to Boston with a new railroad line, making miles of the loveliest beach on the Eastern Seaboard easily accessible.

Throughout the early 1870s the Seashore Company, as it would later come to be known, bought up over seven hundred acres of virtually untouched coastal property from local farmers, in Kennebunk and across the Kennebunk River in Kennebunkport. The men then divided the land into parcels and sold it back to local folks interested in opening cottages, hotels, and inns. But they didn't sell to just anyone. They wanted to ensure that the Kennebunks first created, and then maintained, a certain exclusivity. They achieved this goal with stringent building codes and high prices for the land parcels. For instance, if you erected a cottage in 1895, it had to cost a minimum of $1,550—a small fortune at that time! When new summer diversions were added to the landscape, they tended to reflect interests of the affluent, like Kennebunk River Clubhouse and the lush, green Cape Arundel Golf Club.

One parcel of Seashore land that was sold off in 1902 was a jut of land called Flying Point. Surrounded on three sides by water, the Point had been a popular picnicking and fishing destination, with amazing views of the coast running both north and south, two coves, a small fishing and wading pond, an old walking trail, and wild blueberry patches and juniper bushes. Villagers and longtime summer residents alike were disturbed by the news that the Point had been sold, even though it was sold to longtime summer visitor G. H.

Walker. President George Herbert Walker Bush's grandfather had been bringing his family to Kennebunkport since the early 1880s and began immediately building on the Point. By summer's end, the carpenters had fashioned seventeen railroad cars of lumber into two cottages ready to be occupied. Since then Walker's Point has grown into a massive compound with a pool, tennis courts, and plenty of room for the Secret Service details. There is no public access to the Point, but

Published by Geo. Bonser & Son   Breakwater Court, Oceanic and Cliff Hotels, Kennebunkport, Me.

The towering hotel giants of Kennebunkport, circa 1918. Of the three, only the Breakwater Court, called The Colony now, remains.

"Bushwatchers," as the locals call them, line Ocean Avenue throughout the summer, binoculars dangling around their necks, waiting for a glimpse of the first family.

By the time my family came to the Kennebunks in 1918, the area had already experienced several peaks as a popular resort, and another really hearty tourism boom was just starting. Vacationers flocked to the coast, and in a few years many of Kennebunk's neighboring towns had been nearly ruined by overdevelopment. Instead of the quaint fishing villages they had been, towns took on a carnival atmosphere. In an effort to draw as many families as they could, developers laid down boardwalks, opened casinos and dance halls, and built arcades, amusement parks, and water slides. But the Kennebunk and Kennebunkport areas, thanks to the Seashore Company, eschewed the more commercial, pedestrian attractions of resort life and still do.

TRADITIONAL CHOWDERS

CHOWDERS ARE THE PERFECT WINTER FOOD, PROVIDING WARMTH FOR THE BODY AND COMFORT FOR OUR PSYCHES. That said, it can be ninety degrees on a New York summer day and people will be sitting at Pearl Oyster Bar, slurping down hot chowder. That's when most of my chowder eating takes place too, although it's when I'm on vacation in Maine.

Thick or thin, milk or cream, these are the age-old questions for chowders. I prefer a slightly thicker soup, so I use cream. Milk-based chowders are thought by some to be a more traditional type of chowder, because it's said that cream steps on the flavor of the clam. Since I use a fair amount of the clam broth that comes from cooking the clams, this isn't a problem. Often milk chowders are thickened too, and I'm not crazy about using thickeners. Also cream reduces, so you can control the thickness of the chowder by simmering it for a few minutes more or less.

New England chowder purists swear that chowders must be cured before eating, meaning they must age to attain their optimum flavor—a day or two even, some say. However, you'll get perfectly good results making your chowder just a few hours before you're ready to serve it. Since aging doesn't hurt the chowder, it's a great dish for entertaining because it can be made in advance.

As for the clams, quahogs, the traditional chowder clam, give you more yield with less work. Smaller clams are more tender, but they take longer to shuck. At Pearl, we chop our quahogs fine and add them last, which makes for less chewy bites as you eat the chowder. With scallops, it's more a matter of price. Don't spend too much money buying enormous sea scallops—medium-size scallops will work fine.

Another note about chowders—or soups and stews, for that matter: It's an important cooking technique to add each ingredient separately and season each lightly with salt. This allows the ingredients to be incorporated for a period of time, coaxing maximum flavor out of each ingredient and giving you a better end product.

Clam Chowder

Serves 4

8 pounds fresh quahogs or cherrystone clams

$1/4$ pound double-smoked bacon, diced

1 teaspoon cooking oil

1 large onion, chopped

2 large white potatoes, peeled and cut into $1/2$-inch dice

1 cup clam juice, or reserved strained cooking liquid

3 cups heavy cream

Kosher salt and freshly ground black pepper

Chopped chives

Ideally, you should steam the clams yourself and not buy them in a can. To steam the clams, put them in a pot with a tight-fitting lid and a couple of cups of water. The process takes 3 to 5 minutes, depending on the size of the clam. As with any shellfish, as soon as the shell is open, it's done. Reserve the broth for the chowder.

To make the chowder, in a 4- to 6-quart saucepot, render the bacon in the oil over medium heat. Add the onion and sauté until it is translucent, about 5 to 8 minutes. Add the potatoes, stirring occasionally, and sauté for 3 minutes. Stir in the clam broth, reduce the heat to low, and simmer for 25 minutes. Stir in the cream and simmer for another 25 minutes, until the potatoes are tender. Add the clams and simmer for 5 more minutes. Add salt and pepper to taste.

Ladle the chowder into bowls and sprinkle with the chopped chives. Serve with oyster crackers.

Wet vs. Dry Scallops

Always buy "dry" scallops. I don't even think "wet" scallops, which are cheaper and more prevalent than dry scallops, should be sold. Wet scallops get their name because they are preserved with a chemical called tripolyphosphate. My fish purveyors know never to send me wet scallops, but on the odd chance someone tries to slide some by me, I can always smell the preservative as soon as I put my nose to the fish.

Wet scallops never caramelize when you sauté them because they are filled with liquid. So this beautiful scallop, so full of promise, comes out looking not much darker than it did to start with. Verify with your fishmonger or grocer that you are getting dry scallops. If you haven't developed a relationship with your fishmonger, and you're not sure you're getting dry scallops, look at them closely. If they are glistening, pure white, almost translucent, and swollen, throw 'em back! When you smell them—and you should always smell whatever fish you're buying—there will be a faint metallic or medicinal smell. If the scallops you're looking at are darker white to ivory, or even have a pale flesh-colored cast, and smell a little sweet and of the sea, then they are dry scallops.

Scallop Chowder with Pernod and Thyme

Serves 4

1 tablespoon butter
1 large Spanish onion, finely chopped
2 large white potatoes, peeled and cut into 1/2-inch dice
1 pound dry sea scallops (see Box), cut into 1-inch chunks
1 quart heavy cream
1/4 cup Pernod
1 teaspoon chopped fresh thyme
Kosher salt and freshly ground black pepper
Chopped chives

In a large saucepan over low heat, melt the butter. Add the onion and sauté until translucent, about 5 to 8 minutes. Stir in the potatoes and cook for 2 minutes. Add the scallops and cook for 2 minutes, stirring frequently. Add the cream and simmer for 35 to 40 minutes, or until the potatoes are tender. During the last 10 minutes of cooking time, add the Pernod and thyme and season with salt and pepper to taste. If the chowder seems a little too thick at this point, thin it with a little milk. Ladle it into bowls and sprinkle with the chopped chives.

Oyster Pan Roast with Horseradish Toast

Serves 2

1 tablespoon butter

$1/4$ cup finely diced celery root

$1/4$ cup finely diced parsnip

Kosher salt

$1/2$ cup amontillado sherry

$1^1/2$ cups heavy cream

10 oysters, shucked and reserved in their liquor

Freshly ground black pepper

Horseradish Toast (recipe follows)

In a 10-inch saucepan over low heat, melt the butter. Add the vegetables and sauté until they are slightly softened, about 3 minutes. Add a pinch of salt. Deglaze the pan by stirring in the sherry and cook, stirring, until the sauce is reduced to about 2 tablespoons. Add the cream and reduce again by about two thirds. Stir in the oysters and their liquor and season to taste with salt and pepper. Oysters take only about a minute to poach: their edges will curl slightly when done.

Lift the oysters and vegetables from the pan with a slotted spoon and divide them into shallow soup bowls. Pour in the hot liquid and top with horseradish toast.

Horseradish Toast

Fresh horseradish can be purchased at most specialty food stores. The horseradish root should be firm and not flabby. Peel it as you would a carrot and grate it on the fine side of a box grater, against the grain of the root. Use it immediately, as it will discolor. Leftover horseradish can be stored, covered with white vinegar, in the refrigerator; it will keep about one week.

8 tablespoons (1 stick) unsalted butter, softened
2 tablespoons freshly grated horseradish
Salt and pepper
Ficelle or baguette, cut into $1/4$-inch slices

In a small bowl, mix the softened butter and horseradish. Add a pinch or two of salt and pepper. Refrigerate the mixture until firm. Lay the slices of bread on a cookie sheet. Toast the bread in a 450°F oven for 2 to 3 minutes on each side, until golden brown. Add the horseradish butter to each side for the final minute or so of toasting. Serve immediately with the oyster pan roast.

Pan roasts are a traditional New England dish that can be made from just about any shellfish. I think scallops, lobster, or shrimp work particularly well, and this same recipe can be used for any of these, simply by adjusting cooking time for your choice of shellfish.

East vs. West

The Beard House on West Twelfth Street in Greenwich Village, the home of the late culinary icon James Beard, now houses the James Beard Foundation. One of the ways they raise money is by inviting chefs from all over the country to cook benefit dinners. A few years ago, my friend Mildred Amico, the Beard House's indomitable program director, asked me to put together an oyster dinner for their series. Among the dishes I decided to make was an Oyster Pan Roast. The oysters were to be supplied by someone who was doing a raw oyster tasting before our three-course dinner. This man hailed from the West Coast and espoused the virtues of East Coast oysters grown on the West Coast. Confused? I was too. They were supposed to ship us blue points—an East Coast oyster—that were grown on the West Coast. At the last minute, they substituted an indigenous Pacific oyster. I made a test batch of the pan roast and found that the oysters didn't lend themselves to the dish. The oysters were fat, buttery, and creamy, as were the rest of the ingredients, so the dish didn't work. Ultimately I found that the briny oysters of the East Coast were the perfect counterpoint for a pan roast or stew.

PART TWO

My Grandmother

A Scottish-Jewish Suffragette

MORE THAN ANYONE ELSE IN THE FAMILY, MY GRANDMOTHER WAS THE ONE WHO LOVED THE KENNEBUNKS, THAT IS, UNTIL MY MOTHER CAME ALONG, AND MUCH LATER, ME. From the moment Pearle arrived, whether she was there with her family or all by herself (as occasionally happened in later years), she was content to just sit on the beach and knit, the needles moving so fast they hypnotized the seagulls sitting nearby.

Pearle didn't have much experience with the beach when she was growing up. She was born Rebecca Stein in England in 1896, shortly after the family left Russia. There were eight children by the time my great-grandparents finally finished, including brothers Myer and Pasach (Phillip) and the sisters to whom Pearle was closest, Mady, Mabel, and Katy. Because my grandmother never discussed this time, there are only clues as to where they may have lived in Russia—the first being that they were anxious to get out.

A Stein family portrait taken in Great Britain, circa 1900. Pearle is the second from left.

The second clue is really no more than the history of the time. By the end of the 1800s, Imperial Russia had been notoriously brutal to Jews for decades. Those lucky or resourceful enough to survive the deadly pogroms of the 1870s and 1880s were restricted to living in the overcrowded, economically void urban areas of the Pale of Settlement. Located in the west on the Austro-Hungarian border, wedged between the Black and Baltic Seas, the Pale made up less than 4 percent of the then sweeping Imperial Russian Empire. But more than 95 percent of the Russian and formerly Jewish population was crammed into it. In 1891, when my great-grandparents still would have been in Russia, twenty thousand Jews were forced from Moscow into the Pale. That same year, two thousand were deported to the Pale from St. Petersburg, many of them in chains.

Pearle's father, Abraham, was an auctioneer by occupation, and pictures from her childhood, taken after the family left Russia, indicate a certain wealth. But their trip to freedom, ultimately ending in Brooklyn, New York, was protracted, taking place in several segments over many years. They managed to get to England first, where Pearle was born, and then on to Glasgow, Scotland, where they had close relatives and spent several years before coming to New York.

Although 80 percent of her life was spent in America, she always spoke warmly of her years in Glasgow. From the time I was a teenager, I always referred to her as my Scottish-Jewish grandmother, mostly, I think, because she considered herself more Scottish than anything else. She loved the hilly countryside with the heather riding the knolls in pinkish-purple waves and the light as it fell across the glen at dusk. The city of Glasgow was modern, on the cutting edge of art and design, and perfect for an aspiring performer. Scotland was really the only part of her childhood that she

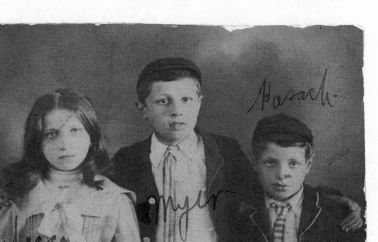

A postcard of Pearle and her brothers from around 1906.

ever discussed with us, and each autumn, when the Manhattan greenmarkets set out pots of heather on their flower stands, I think instantly of my grandmother.

The middle girl, she seemed closer to her brothers Myer and Pasach, to whom she was nearest in age, well into the first years of her marriage. As she got older, however, the age gap between her and her sisters seemed to close, and in later years they were very close. Even as a child, Pearle was a strength to the family, not prone to petty arguments and jealousies, though stubborn and very self-reliant.

When her family moved to New York City, the world began to open up for my grandmother. A beautiful girl in her mid-teens with long dark hair and luminous green eyes, she had grown into a lovely young woman, poised and quiet. In pictures she was petite, although she seemed much taller to me because of her strong character.

In 1913, when my grandmother was seventeen years old, the Women's Suffrage Movement was heating up again in this country. The old guard, Elizabeth Cady Stanton and Susan B. Anthony, had died in 1902 and 1906, respectively, and there was no one with their political weight to take over. It had been more than fifty years since the historic meeting at Seneca Falls, and except for a few states that individually ratified the vote for women, we were no closer than we had been.

Then a radical element began to surface, led by Alice Paul, who had been training in the more militant British Suffrage Movement. Suffragettes circulated petitions around the country, and when one with half a million signatures on it arrived at Congress, the old boys' club was shocked. Marches and protests were prominent in Washington, D.C., and New York City through 1915, and thousands of women took to the streets to march for the vote. In solidarity, they dressed entirely in white: hats, gloves, ankle-length dresses, corsets, bloomers, stockings, and shoes. My grandmother joined them waving a pennant and wearing a sash across her chest, much in the manner beauty queens later would. The sashes, placards, and pennants they carried said

Womens Suffragette parade

July 1 1913 Jessy Levine + me!

A postcard of my grandmother when she was seventeen years old, with her good friend Jesse Levine, at one of the famous Right to Vote parades of 1913.

VOTES FOR WOMEN in the suffrage colors of gold and purple. Spectators by the tens of thousands lined the streets for these marches. The audience included bemused men, women too afraid to march who nevertheless wanted to show their support, and antisuffragists who threw rotten food at the marchers and menaced them in other ways.

My grandmother and her friends took this new movement to heart. They were fearless with the understanding that this was their future, and being able to vote was only part of what they had to gain. If they were to win, they knew that women would be viewed as more complete citizens and that perception alone would have far-reaching ramifications. My grandmother marched and protested every chance she got and, I believe, thought it was a wonderful adventure. My mother and I found saved among her things a beautiful postcard from a 1913 suffrage march she attended. At the time, postcards with your picture on them from wherever you visited were popular souvenirs. This one had a picture of my grandmother and her friend Jesse Levine posing on the back of a cardboard cutout of the Twentieth Century Limited.

In 1916, the movement unified its fractious elements to push a suffrage amendment through Congress. They finally passed the nineteenth Amendment in 1919 and sent it to the states. Tennessee ratified it by a single vote, and on August 26, 1920, seventy-two years after Seneca Falls, nearly a decade after Pearle had become a suffragette, three years after she had been married, and just three years before my mother was born, women finally had the right to vote.

Goldie

Some might consider my grandfather's life the quintessential New York experience for a young Jewish boy in the early part of the twentieth century. Both Goldie's father and grandfather had been in the *schmatta* business, manufacturing baby clothes at their Brooklyn factory. Goldie, Sam, and his sisters, Flora and Minna, had all been born and raised in *the neighborhood*. In this case, the neighborhood was a section of Brooklyn Heights where thousands of Jewish families settled after emigrating from various countries in Eastern Europe.

A charming young fellow with an easy smile and a robust sense of humor, Goldie made friends easily. Athletic and a terrific student, he went off to Cornell University in 1913, at age seventeen, and flourished at the demanding Ivy League school in the bucolic upstate town of Ithaca, New York.

Goldie was quite popular on campus, with his cherubic good looks, sweet smile, and dark hair.

My grandfather, Goldie, in his room at Cornell University, circa 1914.

Besides excelling at his studies, my grandfather enjoyed a regular round of parties and dances, luncheons, and school clubs. One of his most prized possessions was the Cornell scrapbook he put together, which was packed with invitations and programs, snippets from the college paper, pictures, and other memorabilia from what was one of the happiest times of his life.

In 1914, his sophomore year, Myer Stein, a college mate of Goldie's, invited his sister, Rebecca, to visit for the weekend. Myer was not exactly setting up eighteen-year-old Rebecca with Goldie, but he did think they might like one another. In letters to Pearle during this time, Goldie laments on why she would even want someone like him: ". . . positively ugly in face, I can't sing, I can't dance, in fact I can do none of the things which are supposed to attract girls." Their courtship lasted three years, even through the upheaval of Goldie moving back home without his degree.

The Great War had been hard on the once booming family business, Goldsmith's Infants' Long and Short Coats, and as money grew increasingly tight, Goldie had to struggle to stay at Cornell. In 1916, his junior year, he lost the battle and, devastated, came home on his father's order to help in the family business. Because he was older, Sam had managed to avoid this fate and finished his degree at New York University just before the money ran out.

With his Cornell education wrested from his grip, my grandfather's prospects were suddenly dim, as were my grandmother's hopes of marrying Goldie, who was now less suitable in her father's eyes (information suggests that the Steins were considerably more comfortable than the Goldsmiths). Goldie's letters from that year to both Pearle and her father have a pleading tone, as he tries to assure Mr. Stein that he is still an honorable man, capable of caring for his daughter. At the same time, he tells Pearle he will understand completely if she goes off and doesn't look back. My grandmother's return letters make it clear, however, that not only is he still the man for her, but that she is prepared to run the gauntlet of her father for him. But then, as her soon-to-be husband noted in a letter to Mr. Stein in 1914: *I could go on talking all day about Becky. . . . She alone has all the qualities that the girl of my dreams had. . . . She has a will and a mind of her own. She has her moods and her passions. But that is what I have always hoped to see in the girl who would eventually become my wife. She is the kind to help a man when he is down and out—the kind to cheer him in adversity and to share his successes. . . . I hope Myer has the great good-fortune that has come to me.*

Caviar Sophisticates

Pearle and Goldie were married in 1917, when they were both twenty-one. Finances being as dismal as they were, they were forced to move in with Goldie's family—clearly a source of tension between family members, if not my grandparents themselves.

As with many young couples money was an issue. Goldie realized, of course, that Pearle was used to the finer things in life and as generous a man as he was where his "Becky" was concerned, he was equally frugal for himself. While she was recuperating in Atlantic City, he wrote her long letters, always including how much he had made and spent on himself. Her letters back usually asked for a few more dollars next time and if she could extend her stay a bit longer. But they were well matched. He supported her career and she his.

My grandfather did well, and in short order. As his father's business rebounded, Goldie asked for increasingly appropriate compensation. By 1920, he had moved on, building a career with Jewish social organizations and moving up rather rapidly.

Pearle was a challenge for her husband, her daughter, and even her grandchildren, because she expected life to proceed in a particular way. Usually that way was her own, and she paid close attention to the details, expecting tasks to be executed perfectly. She expected this not just of herself, but of others as well. I share this particular curse, as does my mother, so I see it from all perspectives, and it's safe to say that it caused friction.

Pearle's perfectionism, however, was the kind of thing well suited to the opera world. When she was in her late teens, she had begun training her lovely soprano voice to sing professionally. After she married my grandfather, she pursued her goal even more vigorously. In 1930 she went to work at the Metropolitan Opera House, singing soprano in the chorus and touring the country in various operas. My grandfather was proud of his wife's vocal talent and encouraged her to pursue a music career, even though it meant she would have to be away from home.

Throughout their life together, Pearle and Goldie were comfortable and had an active social life, in large part due to Goldie's fund-raising work. During the 1920s, after the initial hardships that young couples often face, it is safe to say that they had an interesting time. In 1925, when Harold Ross published the first issue of *The New Yorker,* it was for people just like my grandparents. As Ross himself described it, it was a weekly for *caviar sophisticates* that extolled urban 1920s New York City, and what a time it was.

The Jazz Age

RECENTLY I FOUND AN INCREDIBLE PHOTO OF MY GRANDMOTHER FROM WHAT MUST HAVE BEEN HER FIRST VISIT TO KENNEBUNKPORT, IN 1920. She's sitting in a spot that has become a favorite of the Charles women, the very tip of the breakwater at Gooch's Beach. It's really just an enormous promenade of granite rocks that extends out into the Atlantic Ocean and has gotten longer, and more decrepit, over the years. Though it's an old black-and-white photo, yellowed with age, you can see that the sun is shining, the sky is clear, and that Pearle is very happy to be sitting in that spot. But there is something else about that photo, and that is what my grandmother is wearing… or not wearing. In her twenties, she was dressed in what would have been a scandalous outfit just two summers before, a short, one-piece bathing suit with a plung-

Pearle sitting on the rocks in front of the Narragansett, circa 1930. The spot has become my mother's and my favorite.

ing neckline and high-heeled shoes. With her head tossed back in a captivating manner, her shoulders and thighs uncovered, and an unabashed smile, Pearle was now a "modern"; she was a new kind of woman for a new era. Able to vote for a president and wear skirts at the knee, she could even enjoy a cocktail and cigarette in relative public, Prohibition notwithstanding.

My grandparents first drove their shiny black Packard touring car through Kennebunk in very early August 1920. As their car motored around Beach

Avenue, following the curves of the three main beaches—Mother's, Middle, and Gooch's—they would have seen some of the same beautiful old stone cottages, shingled saltboxes, and Victorians lining the road across from the water that I now pass. They most likely made it by early afternoon, when the Atlantic Ocean catches the sun just right, holding on to it, then sending it back skittering across the water. I can imagine Pearle stepping off the running board and running down the tiny path to the cashmere sand of Gooch's Beach.

A natty couple, Pearle would have been wearing her spectator pumps and a travel dress, probably white linen with a short pleated skirt and a dropped waist. My grandfather would have been in his cream linen suit with a pale tie, perhaps wearing knickers, which were all the rage and of which he was quite fond. In anticipation of a long, lovely summer at the seashore, the car was loaded down with bathing costumes, beach umbrellas, books, tennis racquets, and knitting supplies for Pearle. As they looked left and right down the beach, they saw handsome young men in belted, striped bathing tanks, pretty flappers in revealing bathing suits, high heels, and full makeup, and happy, bouncing families all enjoying the pleasing combination of soft sand, rugged, rocky coast, and flinty waves. The beach was speckled with enormous, colorfully striped beach umbrellas while jazz music, played on a Victrola, wafted out of a nearby beach house. There was an energy on that beach, just as there was a new kind of excitement breaking across the entire country.

Goldie and Pearle holding my mother. The photo was taken across from Forest Hill, circa 1933.

The Roaring Twenties

My grandparents, their entire courtship and marriage conducted in the shadow of the Great War, had been a part of the original "lost generation": youth disillusioned by the toll the war had taken on their young men and their generation's spirit. The attempt to recapture this spirit ushered in a sexy, glamorous era, the Roaring Twenties, and by decade's end, culture and society had been revolutionized.

From the beginning, the 1920s were about change, about moving beyond the limitations of the past, new opportunities, and new places. When young couples like Pearle and Goldie went out for the evening, they danced the Shimmy, the Blackbottom, or the Charleston instead of waltzing. If they wanted cocktails at home, it meant a trip to the local bootlegger, but if they wanted a drink out, it meant taking your chances at the local speakeasy.

Flappers may have been the figureheads of the era, but it was Prohibition that was the ship, defining the entire decade. Every time Goldie and Pearle met friends out at a speakeasy or juke joint, it meant walking into an establishment that probably had ties to some very nefarious people. Any minute police not on the take could bust in and close the place down, and my grandparents would have been arrested for the simple act of buying a cocktail. But Prohibition meant excitement for a generation craving thrills, and that edge of controlled danger defined the entire decade.

My grandparents were young at a time when every aspect of the world—morality, politics, art, literature, and social consciousness—was changing at a rapid pace. The most celebrated Americans—the ones newspaper boys screamed about on city corners and who captured the imaginations and hearts of the country—were those who took chances. Explorer Richard E. Byrd became the first man to fly over the North Pole, while a young Gertrude Ederle earned a ticker tape parade down New York City streets for being the first woman to swim the English Channel. The feats of magician Harry Houdini and work of archaeologist Howard Carter, who discovered King Tut's tomb in 1922, captivated Americans. But the man who would be the decade's

greatest hero (and the next decade's greatest tragic figure after the kidnapping and murder of his baby son) was aviator Charles "Lucky Lindy" Lindbergh, who risked his life completing the first solo transatlantic airplane flight.

Americans were decades away from having televisions and still a few years away from owning radios, and only the motion picture industry, still in its infancy and literally without voice, captured the country's new joie de vivre. Films captivated my grandmother just as they later would my mother and me. Even when Pearle was on vacation in Kennebunkport, she saw everything she could. The local theater in Dock Square changed their movies nearly every day, showing a glorious rotation of Douglas Fairbanks Sr., Gloria Swanson, and Louise Brooks, Hollywood's "It Girl" and the embodiment of what every young flapper wanted to be: alluring, madcap, and wantonly sexual.

Thoroughly Modern

Flappers were the social icons of the era, their style immortalized by artists and their mores by author F. Scott Fitzgerald. They bobbed their hair, lit cigarettes, and shortened their hemlines, which just a few years before were down around their ankles. They wore rayon stockings and folded them over their garters so that a stiff breeze might expose the back of a bare knee. They rouged their cheeks and painted their lips startling shades of red.

Today flappers seem incredibly feminine with their big made-up eyes, long pastel gowns, and strands of pearls. At the time, though, their look was considered sordid and deviant, because it was devoid of traditional femininity. Dubbed *Garçonne,* or "little boy," the look came directly from the salon of

French designer Coco Chanel. Breasts were bound with bandages so that they appeared flat, and hair was cut increasingly short through the decade, from the "bob" to the "shingle," then covered with cloche hats. Waists dropped to the hipbone and hemlines rose to the knee. There were no more layers of underclothes beneath long heavy skirts, no more pantaloons and corsets. In 1920, my grandmother was enjoying her youth, caught somewhere between playing the flapper and being the respectable young wife.

The biggest change in the young women known as flappers was their attitude: carefree and sexual. After the war, what few young men came home were jaded by watching friends die in foreign lands. They wanted mindless fun and high times. In that atmosphere, young women were not content to wait for happiness to find them. Instead, they were determined to live the same way. They rushed into the job market and, just like men looking for work, moved to big cities as fast as they could. They wore hip flasks, went to petting parties, and drank the gin martinis their slats—flapperspeak for young men—bought them. In 1929, the Great Depression assured that the carefree days were gone, and although zealous flappers fell out of style, the independence they brought with them changed women forever. Throughout the years of the Jazz Age, though, the country was on a heady, wicked ride fueled by bathtub gin, jazz music, and a new open sexuality.

Rum Row

There's a wonderful scene in Fitzgerald's *The Great Gatsby,* in which Jay Gatsby's nemesis, Tom Buchanan, rolls up a bottle of booze in a towel and smuggles it into a room at the Plaza Hotel. He, Daisy, Gatsby, Nick, and Jordan turn it into mint juleps and spend an uncomfortable cocktail hour as the wheels of Gatsby's demise are put in motion. But this is more than a scene in a book. Prohibition left people little choice, and if you wanted to make sure you could have a drink, you had to bring the drink with you.

I don't know exactly how my grandparents managed to get their alcohol during Prohibition, but I know they never went without. Finding a connection in New York City couldn't have been that hard, and my grandfather knew whom to speak with about getting the occasional bottle at home or getting into the local speakeasies with my grandmother and their friends. For Uncle Sam, who lived in Chicago, a hotbed of rum-running activity where gang wars over ter-

Right to left, Pearle, Elaine, Jeanette, and Perle's sister Mabel resting on the running board, circa 1935.

ritory waged weekly, it was probably even easier. But as August 1920 drew near, Sam and Goldie both worried about how to handle libations and their vacation in Maine.

Questions flew back and forth by mail. Should they try to get something when they got up to the Kennebunks or just have a vacation filled with club soda and ginger ale? Not that anyone in the family was a heavy drinker, but like other young people of the times, they enjoyed a cocktail, especially when they were supposed to be relaxing on vacation. But making a reliable connection was the hard part, and who knew how much harder the police might be on folks from out of town if they got caught? Buying alcohol from a stranger meant taking huge risks. So it was decided that, like a scene out of *The Great Gatsby,* my grandfather would buy the cocktail supplies for the summer and bring them up to Maine, since he had the shorter trip and fewer people in his car. Everything would be carefully wrapped so nothing broke— the pungent smell of almost any liquor was an immediate giveaway—and then hidden under something innocent.

Forbidden Fruit

"As goes Maine, so goes the rest of the union." At least that's what they used to say in political circles in the 1800s as the country started to follow Maine into the pit of temperance. In 1851, the sale of liquor was outlawed throughout the state, with Massachusetts and several other neighboring states following their lead.

In 1885, Maine was once again at the forefront of Prohibition legislation, outlawing the making, selling, and drinking of liquor in the state constitution. The rest of the country was slower to follow this time, but the Eighteenth Amendment was finally submitted in 1917 and ratified two years later, in January 1919. One year later, the Volstead Act put Prohibition into effect.

Never were there laws so sure to be broken as those that accompanied Prohibition. As much as the influenza outbreak of 1918 helped temperance, enabling ministers to blame the sin of drinking for the terrible retribution of 540,000 dead (the equivalent of 1.5 million today), World War I worked against it. With nearly an entire generation of young men dead in a war, a bitter and jaded youth was left behind. They had been in foxholes in the Verdun with the kaiser breathing down their young necks, and if they wanted a glass of gin, they were going to have it. Alcohol was forbidden fruit, and being denied just made it more desirable. It is estimated that the more than fifteen thousand bars and clubs that existed before Prohibition exploded to more than thirty-five thousand speakeasies during Prohibition. Some estimates put that number even higher. Nothing really worked about Prohibition. Everybody drank, and crime syndicates and dishonest police officers got rich from the manufacture, transport, and service of liquor.

My grandparents needn't have worried about finding liquor when they visited Maine, since the state was one of this country's major booze smuggling portals. It came by land, over the border, and by water on rum-running skiffs built by Maine craftsmen or commercial vessels from Canada, Newfoundland, and the West Indies.

Rum Row, a string of ships bobbing safely in international waters just three miles from the New England coast, stood sentry from Cape Cod on up into Maine. (On the West Coast, they stood up and down the Pacific.) Rumrunners would dart out across the water on starless, pitch-black nights, load the booze onto their boats, and then motor back to an appointed meeting place on the beach, sometimes in a protected cove or craggy outcropping of rocks. Millions of dollars' worth of European and Canadian liquor made it in this way. Often a diversion in another part of town would be started to make it, literally, smooth sailing for the small boats. Money exchanged hands and the alcohol went to regular citizens, speakeasies, and kitchen bars.

Because of the difficulty in making and storing it, my grandparents didn't have access to ice in a Kennebunk boardinghouse in the 1920s. They gathered in either my grandparents' room or Uncle Sam and Aunt Jenny's and while the men mixed the drinks, the women laid out a plate of boxed crackers and local farmer's cheese that had to pass for hors d'oeuvres. I have often wondered if they were worried about the noise from the cocktail shaker or the distinctive smell of bourbon escaping. I am sure my grandmother scolded them so they wouldn't spill anything on the carpets, and then washed everything thoroughly. They were by no means the only ones having private cocktails in their rooms. Nearly everyone else there was too, and if they weren't, it was because they didn't have the good sense to bring along their own stash. These clandestine cocktail hours were remembered with much fondness in later years, as we sat around the parlor of the Forest Hill House and listened to their stories. Even now I can picture my grandparents elegantly turned out, walking down a dimly lit back alley, and disappearing behind some speakeasy door into the underground nightlife of the 1920s.

COCKTAIL HOUR

AFTER BOURBON MANHATTANS, MY GRANDPARENTS DISCOVERED SIDECARS, A SWEET-TART COMBINATION OF LEMON JUICE, COINTREAU, AND COGNAC THAT MY MOTHER BROUGHT HOME FROM THE NIGHTCLUBS OF NEW YORK IN THE GLITTERING, ROMANTIC LATE 1940S. Then in her early twenties, my mother and her friends were influenced by the elegance of the clubs they went to on Broadway, the drinks and dresses, manners and style. Pearle became quite partial to Sidecars, which she served in her silver goblets that shimmered behind a layer of condensation. In later years, along with champagne, Sidecars definitely usurped the place of the Manhattan as our traditional family drink.

Even now, when I go to Connecticut to have dinner with my mom, we start with an old-fashioned cocktail hour. She puts out a platter of chilled shrimp or my grandmother's chopped liver, and I make a shaker of icy Sidecars or martinis with olives and onions. For us, the cocktail hour is a time to catch up on the events of our lives in a gentle, refined manner. At first my mother, who still works as a reporter with the *New York Times* real estate and Connecticut sections, may discuss what she's writing, and I discuss the restaurant business. As we relax, talk of work evaporates, and we find much more interesting things to say to one another.

Manhattan

1¹⁄₂ ounces Maker's Mark bourbon

¹⁄₂ ounce sweet vermouth

1 maraschino cherry

Sidecar

1 ounce Hennessey Cognac

1 ounce Cointreau

1 ounce lemon juice

Martini

2 ounces Stolichnaya Vodka or Bombay Gin

3 drops dry vermouth

Cocktail olives or onions, or both

Always for martinis, but also for the Sidecar and the Manhattan, a good chill is the key element. I like to put the shaker in the freezer before I make these and keep it there if there is more than enough for a first round. Put enough ice in the shaker to get everything nice and cold but not so much that it will dilute the drink. Pour the liquids in and shake vigorously. Pour the respective drinks into their glasses and garnish.

A Perfect Shrimp Cocktail

The key to a really great shrimp cocktail is attention to detail. My grand-mother and mother were making shrimp cocktails long before I was born, but it wasn't until I started cooking that I realized how much better it tasted when it was boiled in the shell and peeled afterward. The shell imparts a wonderful flavor to the shrimp, in the same way cooking meat on the bone does. Also, seasoning the water makes a great deal of difference. However, if you don't have the seasoning spice for the water, using lemon and parsley will work well too.

4 to 5 16–20–size shrimp per person (see Note)
1/4 teaspoon Bell's seasoning, or lemon and parsley
Charles' Cocktail Sauce or Pearl Oyster Bar cocktail sauce (page 40)
Lemon wedges
Flat-leaf parsley

Note: Size 16–20 refers to the number of shrimp you get per pound. This is the best size for shrimp cocktail as far as I'm concerned—not too big or too small.

There are all sorts of instruments of destruction made for deveining shrimp, but a simple paring knife is the most effective tool. To clean the shrimp, hold it between your thumb and forefinger. Place the point of the knife under the shell at the head of the shrimp, sharp side up. Slide the knife in about 2 inches and bring it straight up sharply so it slices open the back of the shell. Rinse the vein out under a light trickle of water.

To cook the shrimp, in a saucepot, bring 2 quarts of water to a rapid boil. Add the seasoning or lemon and parsley. Drop in the shrimp and cook for about 3 minutes, or until the shrimp is no longer translucent where you deveined it.

Drain the shrimp and plunge them immediately into an ice water bath to stop the cooking. Peel them and, leaving the tail section intact, store them in the refrigerator, covered, until you are ready to use them.

Arrange the shrimp on a platter or in individual parfait glasses, and serve with cocktail sauce, lemon wedges, and flat-leaf parsley.

Combination Cocktail

Serves 1

2 shucked oysters (page 42)

2 shucked littleneck clams (page 43)

2 cooked shrimp, chilled and peeled, tail left on

$1/2$ lobster tail and 1 claw, picked and chilled (page 166)

Pearl Oyster Bar Cocktail Sauce (recipe follows)

Lemon wedge

Place the oysters and clams in the bottom of a parfait glass. Arrange the shrimp on the rim. Cut the lobster tail into chunks and add it to the glass. Use the claw as garnish, so that it's sticking out of the top of the glass. Serve with cocktail sauce and a lemon wedge on the side.

Cocktail Sauces

We can't remember who first made the Charles Cocktail Sauce, my mother or grandmother, but we still make it every time we have shrimp, which is what it goes best with. If you have any left over, it's great on turkey or roast beef sandwiches (because, yes, it's very similar to Russian dressing). I use a more traditional cocktail sauce in the restaurant, with a little chili sauce for an extra kick.

Pearl Oyster Bar Cocktail Sauce

Makes about 1 cup

1/2 cup Heinz chili sauce
1/4 cup Heinz ketchup
1 tablespoon freshly grated (or bottled) horseradish
Squeeze of fresh lemon juice
Pinch of kosher salt and freshly ground black pepper

Whisk the ingredients together in a small bowl. Chill.

The Charles Cocktail Sauce

Makes about 1 cup

1/2 cup Hellman's mayonnaise
1/4 cup Heinz ketchup
1 teaspoon freshly grated (or bottled) horseradish
1 tablespoon finely chopped white onion
Pinch of kosher salt and freshly ground black pepper
1/2 teaspoon chopped Italian parsley

Whisk the ingredients together in a small bowl. Chill.

Clams on the Half Shell

6 littleneck or cherrystone clams per person

1 lemon, cut into wedges

Pearl Oyster Bar Cocktail Sauce (page 40) or Tabasco sauce

Follow the clam shucking instructions on page 43. To serve, place on a bed of crushed ice (if you don't have crushed ice, you can make it in the food processor) on a platter that is a couple of inches deep or a shallow soup bowl and arrange the clams on top. Purists like just a squeeze of lemon on their raw fish, whether it's clams or something else. Others like cocktail sauce or a shake of Tabasco, and still others like to pile everything on.

Oysters on the Half Shell

6 oysters (whatever is freshest at the fish market) per person

Mignonette (recipe follows)

Pearl Oyster Bar Cocktail Sauce (page 40)

1 lemon, cut into wedges

Follow the oyster-shucking instructions on page 42. To serve, layer crushed ice on a platter or shallow soup bowl and arrange the oysters on top. You can put small cups of mignonette and cocktail sauce for dipping on the platter or nearby. At Pearl, I turned shell-shaped mousse molds into inexpensive oyster platters. There's plenty of room for crushed ice, a dozen oysters, lemon wedges, and sauces.

Mignonette

$1/2$ cup red wine vinegar

$1/2$ cup white wine

2 shallots, finely chopped

$1/2$ teaspoon cracked black pepper

~ or ~

$1/2$ cup champagne

$1/2$ cup white wine vinegar

2 shallots, finely chopped

$1/2$ teaspoon cracked black pepper

Mix all the ingredients in a small bowl. Serve with the oysters or clams.

Oyster and Clam Shucking

First, get yourself a good oyster knife. It is as important to the success of this endeavor as your shucking strategy. Don't buy anything really sharp. If you miss while applying a lot of pressure, you're going for stitches. I recommend what the professionals use: a strong, tempered steel blade with an offset tip and a molded white plastic handle.

TO GLOVE OR NOT TO GLOVE: I don't wear a glove while shucking, but I don't wear a seat belt while driving either, so you don't necessarily want to follow my example. Many stores sell a mass-produced shucking glove, which comes in only one size—large. I've seen other gloves made of the inflammable, nontearing material they probably use at NASA, but you can't feel the oyster in your hand while you're working. I find it only makes the job more difficult. For the novice who's just a little nervous about tackling his or her first oyster barehanded, try a fingerless sports glove—the kind weight lifters use. They're made out of leather and are thick enough to withstand a good stab, giving you some protection without sacrificing dexterity.

SHUCKING TECHNIQUES: Okay, now you're armed and ready for action. For the beginner, I suggest small oysters, sometimes referred to as cocktail size, since they are the easiest to open. The larger the oyster, the bigger the muscle, which makes it more difficult to open. Most varieties of oysters are built differently; that is to say, they all have shell characteristics that can affect the degree of difficulty in opening. For instance, Malpeques can be shaped very irregularly, sometimes almost bent in half, which makes the shell often break during opening. Start with something simple such as small bluepoints or Wellfleets. Fisher Islands and Sakonnets are also relatively easy.

Fold a kitchen towel over a couple of times to give yourself a cushion and prevent the oyster from slipping. Place the oyster on it, flat side up. Put the point of the knife into the hinge, wiggling it a little to get in as far as possible. Hold the oyster firmly down with one hand and use leverage on the knife to pop the hinge open. With small oysters, it's all about leverage. The larger ones require strength as well.

Once the hinge is popped open, slide the knife down the side a little, with the tip just inside, and turn the blade up. This will allow you to get inside the oyster to sever the muscles that anchor it to the shell, both top and bottom. Keeping your knife flat against the inside of the top shell, cut the muscle and discard the shell. Now, being careful not to cut the oyster, slide the knife underneath it and sever the bottom muscle.

At the New York Oyster Festival Shucking Competition, shuckers get points off for presenting oysters with cuts, bits of shell or mud, or unsevered muscles. Many people flip the oyster over after shucking so that it has a plumper appearance, but I think when you serve an oyster, it should look as untouched in its shell as possible.

FOR CLAM SHUCKING: Holding the clam in the palm of your hand, line the edge of the knife up with the tiny opening between the two shells. Quickly but carefully slide the knife in about halfway. Pull back the top shell with your thumbs. Using your clam knife, scour the membrane off the top shell so that it rests on top of the clam in the bottom shell. Scour the bottom shell underneath the clam to separate that membrane as well. Pull off the top shell and discard it.

Objectionable Strangers

WHILE THE SEASIDE COMPANY MAY HAVE CREATED A BEAUTIFUL RESORT, THE PROBLEM WITH BEING EXCLUSIVE WAS THAT SOMEONE WAS BEING *EXCLUDED*. As an 1890 travel brochure about Kennebunkport stated: "They have been careful to let none but the elite of cottagers to locate here . . . thus the reputation of the place is not permitted to suffer because of the presence of objectionable strangers."

Although the world was changing quickly, some changes couldn't come quick enough. So, Pearle, Goldie, Sam, and Jenny may have been caviar sophisticates in New York City, but in Kennebunkport they were also the objectionable strangers mentioned in the travel brochure.

In 1920, Kennebunkport was a beautiful, quaint seaside town, with plump, good-natured children playing in the sun and lobstermen working their colorful dories. But behind the picket fences, beyond the county fairs and candy shops, small towns often had a darker side, or perhaps it was just a more naïve side. As optimistic and gay as the 1920s were, they didn't erase the religious and racial prejudice that hovered

The Kennebunkport Goldsmiths circa 1933: (from left) Jenny, Sam, Flora, Pearle, and Sol. In front are the cousins, Marc, Ted, my mom, and Minna's son, George.

around the edges of American society. America was still forty years away from its first Catholic president, and even then the win was considered quite a feat for John F. Kennedy. Certainly more extreme prejudice existed in places with far less reason than an old Yankee fishing village like Kennebunkport, but exist it did.

It was a strange time in America. As much as it was an age of enlightenment in the fields of art, culture, and science, there was a frightening undercurrent. The Ku Klux Klan had a sudden growth spurt across the country and between 1920 and 1924, membership in the group jumped from two thousand to an estimated five million. In fact, the Klan had spread so fast in Maine that *Collier's,* a popular magazine at the time, published an article about it in 1924 called "Maine Gone Mad."

When my uncle and Jenny came to Kennebunkport in 1918, with their Jewish-sounding last name, they were not particularly welcome. Of the more than twenty hotels at Kennebunk Beach, only the Forest Hill House accepted reservations from Jews. Regardless of how friendly, well-dressed, nice-looking, and affluent a family the Goldsmiths were, or how many vacancies there were in town, if you were Jewish your only option was Forest Hill.

Goldie with Ellie.

Mr. Social Work

Into this atmosphere came Uncle Sam and my grandfather who spent their careers, their lives really, working in public service, specifically for Jewish organizations. In my grandfather's long career, he worked for the Federation of Jewish Charities, the American Jewish Congress, the Red Cross War Fund of Greater New York, the Greater New York Fund, and the National War Fund. In 1945, he took his final position as the secretary for financial development for the National Conference of Christians and Jews, a group that worked to promote interfaith understanding. No doubt with his sparkling personality he was able to entice many a philanthropist to donate to these causes.

Uncle Sam worked for so many organizations and served on so many committees that in 1959, when Loyola University honored him, one of many institutions to do so over the decades, it prompted them to call him "Mr. Social Work of Chicago . . . an example of citizenship at its best." He served on the Mayor's Committee on the Relief, was the chairman of the Illinois Public Aid Commission during the Depression, and director of the Jewish Charities of Chicago, among other positions. During the Depression era, he was instrumental in so many institutions to help the poor that they are too numerous to mention.

One of his greatest contributions, however, was getting Jews out of Germany during World War II. The details of these missions are still cloaked in mystery more than fifty years later. What little we do know is that it probably began when Sam helped organize and was asked to serve as the executive director of the Jewish Welfare Fund of Chicago, which raised funds for "European Jews in danger of extermination." Then, when America entered the war, Uncle Sam was stationed overseas, and his involvement in removing Jews from Germany became more active, according to my cousin Louise, Sam's granddaughter. It was while he was a lieutenant colonel supervising the care of countless refugees in Italy that Sam became involved with a group responsible for physically moving Jews out of Nazi-occupied territories.

My mother heard vague references to the story when she was a young woman, but it was Louise who pumped her elderly grandmother, Jenny, for more information. Neither my mother nor Louise was ever able to learn any further details. Louise says that Sam's impressive roster of friends from that time, however, including David Ben-Gurion, the first prime minister of Israel, is some indication of the level at which Uncle Sam was working.

When he returned home in 1945, Sam continued his service to the welfare of others in a slew of social organizations. At the time of his death, in 1987, he was ninety-four and still active as the vice president of the Jewish Federation of Metropolitan Chicago and executive head of the Combined Jewish Appeal and the Jewish Welfare Fund.

A Place to Stay

For years, I could not figure out how in 1918 Uncle Sam managed to find the one hotel in Kennebunkport that accepted Jews. Spending time at Kennebunk's Brickstore Museum, which also houses the collections of a well-tended Kennebunk Historical Society, finally shed some light on what probably happened. When Rosalind "Liz" Magnuson, the head of research for the Brickstore, put together an exhibit entitled *Quiet, Well Kept, for Sensible People: The Development of Kennebunk Beach From 1860–1930,* she researched the history of the local hotels thoroughly. It was during the scouring of local and state libraries, poring over historical diaries, land deeds, and records that Liz found a diary note from another Kennebunk Beach hotel stating that they did not accept reservations from Jews. It went on to say that it was a widespread policy that included most of the hotels in the area, and if families suspected of being Jewish inquired about reservations they were to be sent immediately to the Forest Hill House.

So perhaps on the Nova Scotia trip of 1918, Uncle Sam walked into any hotel in Kennebunkport and introduced himself, or signed the guest register, only to have been politely told that they had no vacancies. Maybe the desk clerk even offered to crank up the telephone and call over to the Forest Hill House to see if there were any vacancies. I can't imagine that Uncle Sam would have been as enamored of a city as he was of Kennebunkport if he had been treated badly.

An Untapped Market

Cora Toothaker had run Forest Hill House since the late 1800s and her decision to seek out a Jewish clientele could not have been one taken lightly. Both she and her husband, David, had to know there would be, at the very least, social consequences. Cora was pragmatic and well-known for being a clever businesswoman, but after nearly two successful decades, national and international events were conspiring against resort towns and their economy.

In 1917, young men were going off to war and not coming back. Money was tight, and families had concerns too serious to think about vacationing at the shore. Then the flu epidemic hit the next year, killing over a half million people in this country. Since Forest Hill had never discriminated, concentrating on a Jewish clientele may have been as easy as accepting more reservations from the friends and family of her guests. She may have just decided to fill what would have been a pretty large void in the local economy—accommodating a clientele of wealthy New York and Boston Jews.

The only advertisement I could find after the 1910s appeared in *The Kennebunkport Times* on June 30, 1917: ". . . Pleasantly located near ocean, river and woodland. Table supplied with the best that market affords. . . . Sanitary conditions perfect. For terms apply to: D. F. Toothaker, Kennebunkport." But with a strong word-of-mouth business and referrals from every other hotel in the area, there would have been no reason for her to advertise once her clientele was established.

At the time, many local newspapers in resort towns devoted space to the events at hotels and inns and printed the hotels' guest lists. The Forest Hill House didn't appear in any of these lists, nor did the traveling acts that Cora booked or the hayrides, dances, clambakes, mah-jongg, and tennis tournaments she held. It is very possible that the Toothakers did not particularly want too much "publicity," deciding to keep a low profile for the safety of their clients. Forest Hill sparkled with witty and wealthy guests in all types of businesses from all over the country. Mrs. Oppenheimer, a well-known and wealthy Jewish philanthropist, stayed there with her family each summer. (In a connection made at Forest Hill, Uncle Sam's oldest son, Mark, ended up working for Mrs. Oppenheimer's nephew, Robert, on the Manhattan Project as a graduate student.) However, not everyone appreciated Forest Hill's charming, accomplished guests.

Dorothy Parsons Christopher, whose mother, May Parsons, bought the Forest Hill House in 1937, says, "Although it was never directed right at us, there was definitely a stigma attached to keeping Forest Hill's Jewish clientele. We knew it." But her family worked hard to make sure it was never felt by their guests.

In the middle of a steamy August night in 1939, when guests and help were sound asleep, someone crept silently around the parking lot and painted enormous white swastikas on all of the guests' cars. At dawn the following morning, when the dew was still on the grass, Rosa the cook was on her way to start breakfast when she was stunned by the vandalism.

On the front lawn at Forest Hill in 1967: Grandma, mom, me in back, and David in front.

She ran to the kitchen to tell May, and they rushed out with buckets of soapy water and rags to clean the cars before the guests woke up. If the purpose had been to scare the owners and staff at Forest Hill, it succeeded for a while, though not enough to change anything. If, on the other hand, it was meant to terrify the guests, it was a failure. To this day, the guests have never found out about the incident.

I'd occasionally hear a story about the prejudice my family came up against in the Kennebunks, but it never registered with me as anything other than a story. When I was a little girl, I knew we stayed at the Forest Hill House because my grandmother had always stayed there. Since she and my mother loved it so, it was absurd to think they would have considered staying anywhere else. My mother says a similar thing. She remembers sitting on the porch after dinner and hearing her parents talk with the other guests about how they found out about Forest Hill and vague references to anti-Semitism. "Even then," she says now, "it was unreal to me. Just a story I heard about something that once happened."

The Forest Hill House

MY FAMILY CAME TO LOVE FOREST HILL AND THE PEOPLE WHO
RAN IT. How often do you find a hotel or inn that everyone in the family adores so much that at least some of them return each summer for the
next six decades? Each year we would come—my grandparents, parents,
brothers and sisters, uncles and aunts, and cousins—with occasional additions to
the pool of regulars. Sam and Goldie's youngest sister, Minna, would come
sometimes, and in later years she would send her son George, who was a bit
younger than my mother. In the 1930s, Pearle's brothers or sisters and their
families would sometimes tag along as well.

The Forest Hill House was a wonderful place to visit. The owners were
well-known for their
delicious meals and
prolific vegetable
gardens. The house
was warm and com-
fortable with spa-
cious rooms that
were always immac-
ulately cleaned. My
grandmother, who
had Bon Ami run-
ning through her
veins, would not

Summer 1928, tiny
guests crowd around
the side door of the
Forest Hill House. My
mother is the little girl
on the far right (with
the flower in her hand).

have tolerated anything less. It was also well priced, as both my mother and
local historians have explained to me. Forest Hill catered to well-off families with
nowhere else to stay, but they never took advantage of that fact.

Although its surrounding landscape had changed much during its first
fifty years, by 1919 the large, exquisite white farmhouse sat on a piece of land

thick with towering pines. Bobwhites and whippoorwills came from all over to nest in the trees, and as they darted around the yards their songs filled the air. A long queue of lilac and honeysuckle bushes, whose branches had spread so wide they must have been growing for decades, ran down the side lawn. Wide vegetable patches sat next to the barn, and by August the once orderly rows were a brightly colored jungle of tomato plants, lettuces, peppers, cucumbers, peas, wax and green beans, carrots, different varieties of squash, and fresh herbs.

Adirondack chairs were grouped around the yard to catch the sun, and behind the house wicker settees sat invitingly under the shade of two weeping willows. Part of the lawn was devoted to a croquet court, and there was a red clay tennis court, as well as horseshoe pits for the gentlemen. My mother's memories of the Forest Hill House start when she was just a toddler. Now eighty, she recalls everything as being bright and airy inside the inn, in marked contrast to the beautiful but dark New York City apartments in which she grew up. A nice, clean place to stay with comfortable and attractive furnishings of the day, the Forest Hill was not, however, luxurious by modern standards in any way.

—◦◦◦—

In 1872, the same year that the Seashore Company incorporated and started selling parcels of land to would-be hotel and cottage owners, a wily Ansel Boothby, Cora's father, bought up the real estate surrounding his farm and began building the Forest Hill House. Set on a plot not far from the land the Seashore Company was developing, it was in a lovely spot, with docks into the Kennebunk River right across Beach Avenue and three beautiful beaches a short walk up the road. The Seashore Company had been conspicuous about what they were doing, and although Ansel had originally planned to build a working farm, Liz Magnuson says there are clues visible in pictures of the original structure that innkeeping may have occurred to him even as the buildings were being erected. The house was large, with many rooms (another building was added in Cora Toothaker's day), and there were plenty of windows, including two enormous bay windows in the front that ran from floor to ceiling on the first floor.

By the mid-1880s, Ansel had turned the Boothby farm into a boarding-house for summer visitors. A blurb about the inn appeared in a July 1887 edition of *The Wave,* the local paper: "The Forest Hill House is expecting a big crowd this August. This cozy little place is becoming very popular with its guests who enjoy home comforts, large cool rooms, and an excellent table."

By the time my grandparents started visiting, the Boothbys were experienced innkeepers who worked hard to please their guests. There were fireworks displays, tennis tournaments, hayrides, canoe picnics, and day trips out to Parsons Beach, Ogunquit, or York, with box lunches packed by Rosa.

Each room had a pitcher and basin set for evening and morning face, hands, and teeth cleaning. Guests kept their doors open at night so that the cool evening breezes could circulate and force the heat of the day from the rooms. White, flowing curtains hung inside the threshold for privacy. There were water closets on each floor and a bathroom with a shower, although showers weren't popular back then. Only one bathroom had a tub, which caused long lines. Nellie, the Toothaker's old chambermaid, saw an opportunity and demanded a fifty-cent "tip" from any guest wanting her to clean out the tub before they used it. Of course, it was more like a toll, and to put its enormity into perspective, the charge for the stay was twelve dollars per week for a family of three . . . and that included three meals a day! With just a few hygiene-obsessed guests, Nellie could almost make as much herself.

From the 1880s through World War I, Forest Hill was a popular hotel with the locals, who often attended dances, vaudeville appearances, and other events there. It had become a standard bearer for hospitality to even the smallest accent. With popularity came growth, and by season's opening in 1892, Ansel had remodeled Forest Hill into a true hotel. The Boothbys built a loyal following of people who returned year after year, and when Cora and David Toothaker took over the inn from her father somewhere just after 1900, it was a seamless change.

Cora Boothby Toothaker

Town elders have vague memories of Cora as an old-time Maine native, pragmatic and defiant. Margery Orem remembers her aunt Cora fondly. "My mother would bring us over, and she was always very sweet to us. Shortly after she sold the inn, I remember visiting her and sitting at her bedside when she was ill. She was still very proper, very put together."

My mother remembers a tall stately woman with long hair swept up in a bun, who was sometimes stern but could often be jolly. But what really made an impression on little "Ellie," who would later become a talented and successful Broadway costume designer, was the way Cora dressed. While most women had embraced the shorter skirts of the Jazz Age, at least to some degree, Cora was still sweeping around the hotel in the long skirts and petticoats of the last century. "She was probably only fifty years old at the time but it's as if she got stuck in the 1890s," laughs my mother. "As hot as it could get from mid-July through late August, Mrs. Toothaker always wore long skirts down to her ankles, corsets with stays, and crisp white shirts with long sleeves and these very high, very starched collars at her neck. Sometimes she even wore the men's-style neckties that were popular for women at the turn of the century or a lace scarf pinned with a large brooch. I don't know how she did it—we didn't have so much as a fan at the Forest Hill House, and she was constantly on the move, overseeing all of the help, making sure her guests were satisfied, looking after a farm. You could hear her skirts rustling as she moved quickly from one part of the hotel to another, from one task to another."

Cora ran the hotel for more than fifty years, through the Great War and the Great Depression. She had run the place alone since David's death in 1929. She may have looked like she was in her fifties to young Ellie, but by the time she retired in July 1937, she was seventy-five years old and the work had just gotten to be too much for her. She left Forest Hill in the capable hands of May Parsons and her husband, and that November Cora moved down to Orlando, Florida. She was taken ill shortly after arriving, and several months later she passed away in a Florida hospital. Only a tiny paragraph in the Kennebunkport newspaper marks her death on March 9, 1938, and doesn't even mention that she was brought home to Kennebunkport and buried in the Boothby family plot, a few hundred feet from the Forest Hill House. At a time when others were too scared, Cora Boothby Toothaker gave hundreds of families the opportunity to have summer memories that have been passed down through the generations.

The Parsons

Dorothy remembers exactly when she learned that her mother, May, bought the Forest Hill House, because it was entwined inextricably with another memory. On July 3, 1937, Dorothy was eight years old and away at summer camp when she got a letter from her mother telling her about Forest Hill. It was the same day the camp radio was reporting that the plane of aviatrix and national heroine Amelia Earhart had gone down somewhere over the Pacific. Dorothy says she now remembers when her mother bought the hotel only because of Earhart's fateful trip.

May Parsons had worked through the summer of 1936 with Cora to train, and, more important, to meet the guests, most of whom came so regularly they were like family. (They would become family to Mrs. Parsons too, who when she died in 1981, still had over twenty Forest Hill guests on her Christmas card list, even though she hadn't owned the hotel for decades. She and my grandmother exchanged season's greetings until Pearle's death in 1978.)

May tried to update the hotel, bringing modern conveniences to her guests without sacrificing the unspoiled innocence of the inn and the value. In 1940, the Parsons turned the dance hall into living quarters for the help and more rooms for guests. May added washbasins with running water in each room and updated the bathrooms.

Then a small disaster struck the Forest Hill House in May 1942, when part of the hotel caught fire. Fires had cost the Kennebunks enormous financial, historical, and physical loss over the years. Between the old wooden structures and frequently strong ocean breezes, an entire village could disappear in a matter of hours, which is exactly what happened to the town of Goose Rocks Beach in 1947.

The Parsons, and Forest Hill, were much luckier than Goose Rocks, and although $20,000 worth of damage was done, the fire was put out relatively quickly. But with Memorial Day approaching, the fire made it impossible to open for the season. What wasn't charred was water damaged, and smoke had invaded everything from the linens to the walls. With a register full of guests whom other hotels were not going to accept, May was worried. There were already fewer rooms available to begin with because World War II gas rationing had closed the bigger glamour hotels across the harbor in the swank part of Kennebunkport. A few years earlier, wealthy vacationers would not travel without a several-car caravan containing their maids, chauffeurs, and other members of their household staff, but those days disappeared with gas rationing, and the wealthy found places closer to home to play.

One of the Kennebunk glamour hotels ended up in the possession of the bank, and sensing an opportunity, bank officials came to May with an idea. They wanted her to bring her guests and staff over to the larger hotel for the summer and run it as if it were the Forest Hill House. A crisis was averted: The Parsons wouldn't go bankrupt and could accept even more reservations, Jewish visitors to the Kennebunks would still have a place to stay, even more jobs would be available for the summer, and an empty property would be used. The only difference for the guests was that the beach was not as accessible and a five-cent ferry ride was required to get across the harbor to the beach. But when May contacted each of her guests by post, there were no complaints, just relief that their vacations were not going to be interrupted.

May busily set about making the new place ready, but less than a week after they started work on it, the gentlemen from the bank paid another call. Certain Kennebunkport citizens had circulated a petition against this invasion, managing to get hundreds of signatures. The locals decided that they did not want Forest Hill's regular guests in their community. May was welcome to accept other guests, they said, but not her Jewish clientele. Shocked that any-one would go to the extent of actually passing around a petition, she angrily tore it up and the guests came anyway. The hotel's accommodations were much more luxurious than Forest Hill, but when the next year came around, they were all happy to be nestled back into their little retreat on Beach Street.

During World War II, business was booming and May helped local fami-lies out by sending her overflow to stay in nearby private homes, who, now that they needed the money, were only too happy to rent a room to Forest Hill's Jewish guests. They would come back to Forest Hill for their three meals and then go to the beach or back to their rooms, which were sometimes blocks away. There were many meals when the dining room was packed to its new 150-person capacity. It was a patriotic time, and the Kennebunks seemed filled with laughter and music. Young sailors walked around town in their "whites" or met young girls at local USO dances sponsored by the local lodge. Big bands, the lesser-known ones anyway, played at clubs in the area, and the town sometimes seemed like it was bursting at the seams.

Many things had been complicated by the war if you were in the hospi-tality business. For one, rationing became increasingly strict, and when my family came to stay, they turned their food rationing coupons over to May, who was responsible for the bookkeeping nightmare all those coupons brought. With labor shortages caused by the war, Dorothy became a reluctant waitress and her dad, a revenuer during Prohibition, became a reluctant cook. Dorothy says her parents expected her to be a role model. "I was held to the highest standards. I stayed in the help's quarters just like everyone else, only I didn't get paid the twenty-five-dollars-a-summer-plus-tips salary. The worst thing was missing out on going to the movies. They were such a big part of life, almost like television is now, and the movie house ran a new movie every night. But we were still working during the first show and our curfew meant we couldn't catch the second show. My parents finally relented and lift-ed curfew so that we could go to the movies twice a week. You know how some kids get homesick when they are at camp? I was homesick *for* camp!"

May and Pearle became quite friendly over the years. My grandmother, like her daughter and granddaughter, was a cat lover, and one year May gave her a beautiful yellow kitten from her cat's annual litter. For the next decade, Dorothy remembers seeing my grandmother walk the cat down the beach each summer. "That was quite a sight, seeing her walking down the beach with the cat on a leash. Pearle was really quite something, just fascinating to be around, especially if you were a kid. She was a striking blonde, and always dressed impeccably, classic but chic. I remember my mother saying that she was one of the stars of the Metropolitan Opera's chorus, one of the people they put out front. The other day I was going through my jewelry box and I found the beautiful pin Mrs. Goldsmith gave me when I was married. It was a bouquet of forget-me-nots and was always one of my favorites. So was she."

THE VEGETABLE PATCH

Roasted Vegetables

PEOPLE SEEM TO THINK ROASTING IS MORE DIFFICULT OR INVOLVED THAN IT IS. In fact, it's the easiest way to cook beets, and in the end you have wonderful vegetables that have had the flavor coaxed from them slowly, producing a sweet, tender vegetable with all of the natural sugars intact.

Beets

Serves 2

1 bunch beets
Sherry vinegar
4 tablespoons ($1/2$ stick) unsalted butter
Kosher salt and freshly ground black pepper
Fresh chives

Preheat the oven to 450°F. Cut off the greens and place the beets in a large roasting pan with 2 inches of water. Cover the pan with foil and roast the beets for 1 hour, or until the beets are soft when pierced with the tip of a knife. Peel and cut them into $1/2$-inch dice.

In a sauté pan over medium heat, heat the beets with 2 tablespoons of water and a splash of sherry vinegar. Reduce the liquid to 1 tablespoon and add the butter. Toss until the butter is incorporated. Remove from the heat or the sauce will break. Season to taste with salt and pepper and garnish with chives. Serve immediately.

Parsnips

Serves 2

4 to 5 fresh parsnips
1 tablespoon clarified butter (see Note)
Kosher salt and freshly ground black pepper
Fresh parsley

Preheat the oven to 450°F. Peel the parsnips, cut them into $1/2$-inch slices on the bias, and place them in a roasting pan with the clarified butter. Roast them for about 10 minutes, turning over once or twice while roasting, until the parsnips are tender. Lightly season to taste with salt and pepper and garnish with a little fresh parsley.

Note: Clarified butter is difficult to make in small amounts, so use at least a pound of unsalted butter, which will yield enough for 4 people if you are serving it with lobster. Melt the butter in a double boiler; you can create one by floating a small pot in a larger pot of simmering water. When the butter is completely melted, skim the top, then slowly pour off the pure golden clarified butter, carefully leaving the milk solids at the bottom. Keep the butter warm until you're ready to use it. Any excess clarified butter can be stored in the refrigerator and used in place of oil for sautéing. It tastes great and can stand high temperatures because it contains no milk fat to burn.

Brussels Sprouts

Serves 2

2 cups brussels sprouts
1 tablespoon clarified butter (see above) or olive oil
2 garlic cloves, sliced
Kosher salt and freshly ground black pepper
Fresh parsley

Preheat the oven to 450°F. Clean and halve or quarter the brussels sprouts. Place them in a roasting pan with the clarified butter and garlic. Roast for about 10 minutes, or until tender. Lightly season to taste with salt and pepper and garnish with a little fresh parsley.

Sugar Snap Peas with Lemon and Toasted Almonds

Serves 4

2 tablespoons sliced almonds

$1/2$ pound sugar snap peas

1 tablespoon unsalted butter

Finely chopped zest of $1/2$ lemon

Kosher salt and freshly ground black pepper

Preheat the oven to 350°F. Place a single layer of almonds on a pie plate and toast for 4 minutes, or until they are light brown. Shake the pie plate two or three times while toasting. Set aside.

In a medium saucepan, bring $1/2$ cup of lightly salted water to a boil. Add the sugar snap peas and blanch for about 1 minute. Pour off all but 1 teaspoon of the water, add the butter and lemon zest, and swirl until mixed to create a beurre fondue. The sauce can break, so take it off the heat as soon as it's completely melted and bubbling. Add the sliced almonds and toss. Adjust the salt and if necessary, add a few grinds of pepper. Remove from the heat and serve.

Roasted Red Pepper Relish

Makes about 1½ cups

In the summer, I like to serve this as an accompaniment for pan-roasted and grilled fish, particularly salmon, tuna, and halibut.

3 red bell peppers

½ cup sun-dried tomatoes

3 Roma tomatoes, seeds removed

1 cup fresh basil leaves, washed, dried, and chopped

3 tablespoons good-quality balsamic vinegar

½ cup extra-virgin olive oil

Kosher salt and freshly ground black pepper

Roast the red peppers on an open gas burner or on the grill, turning them frequently until they are blackened. Place them in a bowl, cover with plastic wrap, and refrigerate until they're cool. Peel, seed, and cut the peppers and tomatoes into uniform small dice. Place the peppers and tomatoes into a large bowl. Stir in the basil, balsamic vinegar, and olive oil. Add salt and pepper to taste. Let the relish macerate for about 1 hour at room temperature.

Summer Caponata

Makes about 3 cups

6 Japanese eggplants

½ cup extra-virgin olive oil

1 large Vidalia onion, diced

4 medium cloves garlic, minced

6 plum tomatoes, cut in half, seeded, and diced

Kosher salt

$1/2$ cup white wine

3 tablespoons balsamic vinegar

2 tablespoons sugar

$1/4$ pound black oil-cured olives (Nyon or Moroccan), pitted and chopped

$1/4$ pound Picholine or good-quality green olives, pitted and chopped

1 tablespoon small capers

5 fresh basil leaves, chopped

Freshly ground black pepper

Preheat the oven to 200°F. Rub 3 of the eggplants with 2 tablespoons of the olive oil. In a large roasting pan, roast them for 45 minutes, or until they are soft. Let them cool, chop them roughly, and set them aside. Quarter the other 3 eggplants lengthwise, then slice them into $1/2$-inch chunks.

In a large sauté pan, heat 3 tablespoons of the olive oil over medium heat and sauté the onion until it is translucent, about 8 to 10 minutes. Add the garlic and sauté for 2 minutes, or until the garlic is golden. Stir in the fresh eggplant chunks and tomatoes, lightly salt, and sauté for 2 minutes. Add the white wine, balsamic vinegar, and sugar and cook for 10 minutes, stirring occasionally, until the vegetables are soft. Add the roasted eggplant, olives, and capers and simmer for 5 minutes. Fold in the basil and the remaining 3 tablespoons of olive oil. Adjust the salt and add several grinds of black pepper. Place the mixture in a bowl and chill until you're ready to use.

Slaws

I'VE ALWAYS LOVED COLESLAWS, USING THEM AS SIDE DISHES FOR EVERYTHING FROM OYSTER ROLLS TO WHOLE GRILLED FISH. Far from the chopped green cabbage with flecks of carrot from our school cafeteria days, the slaw can be quite elegant. I've made slaws out of all sorts of vegetables and by using several different dressings.

Slaws can be savory or sweet, mayonnaise-based or lightened with vinaigrette. Although I am not a proponent of low-fat products, like low-fat or fat-free mayonnaise, they can be substituted. Instead of or in addition to red, white, or green cabbage, try a julienne of any of the following vegetables for slaws: roasted golden or red beets; greens like arugula, dandelion, or mustard; red, yellow, orange, or even hot peppers; red onions; carrots; cucumber; or fennel. For a sweeter slaw, apples, pears, pineapples, mangos, jicama, and papaya work really well. Walnut or hazelnut oils are interesting as well. It pays to experiment.

Celery Root Slaw

Serves 6

4 cups peeled, julienned celery root

1¾ cups Pearl Oyster Bar Tartar Sauce (page 157)

5 tablespoons white wine vinegar

½ teaspoon kosher salt

Pinch of freshly ground black pepper

In a large bowl, blend all the ingredients well. Refrigerate at least 3 hours before serving.

Cabbage Slaw

Serves 6

4 cups julienned Savoy or green cabbage (or 2 cups red cabbage,
    julienned, and 2 cups green cabbage for a more colorful presentation)
1¾ cups Pearl Oyster Bar Tartar Sauce (page 157)
5 tablespoons sherry vinegar
½ teaspoon sugar
½ teaspoon kosher salt
Pinch of freshly ground black pepper

In a large bowl, blend all the ingredients well. Refrigerate at least
3 hours before serving.

Warm Cabbage Salad

Serves 4

I prefer to use green cabbage, since red cabbage leaches color under the
warm dressing.

½ cup walnuts or pecans
1 medium head of green cabbage, thinly sliced
¼ cup white wine vinegar
1 tablespoon sherry wine vinegar
Kosher salt and freshly ground black pepper
½ cup canola oil (or peanut oil)
4 strips double-smoked bacon, julienned before cooking
Chopped flat-leaf parsley

Preheat the oven to 400°F. Toast the nuts on a baking sheet for 5 minutes. In a large salad bowl, toss the cabbage to separate. In a small saucepot, bring the vinegars to a boil. Pour the mixture over the cabbage, lightly salt and pepper it, and toss. Heat the oil in a saucepan over high heat, add the bacon, and cook it until very crispy. Pour the bacon and oil over the salad, add the nuts, and toss well. Adjust the seasoning if necessary. Garnish with chopped parsley.

Corn Pudding

Serves 4

My favorite way to serve this New England pudding is as an accompaniment to a boiled or grilled lobster. When the corn season starts to wane and the corn is not as sweet, it still tastes great in this pudding.

1^1/$_2$ cups corn
4 eggs
2 cups heavy cream
Pinch of grated nutmeg
Kosher salt and freshly ground black pepper

Preheat the oven to 350°F. Purée the corn in a food processor until it's fairly smooth. Add the eggs while it's pulsing, then add the heavy cream and seasonings. Pour the mixture into 3- or 4-ounce ramekins and place the ramekins in a roasting pan. Put the roasting pan in the oven and then pour in enough water to come halfway up the side of the ramekins. Bake for 1 hour, or until set and lightly brown on top. Serve warm.

Sweet Corn Ragout

Serves 6

Kernels from 4 ears of fresh sweet corn

$1/2$ cup fava beans or English peas

2 tablespoons ($1/4$ stick) unsalted butter

3 tomatoes, seeded and diced

Kosher salt and freshly ground black pepper

2 tablespoons chopped fresh basil

2 tablespoons chopped chives

4 basil sprigs for garnish

In a sauté pan, over medium heat, bring $1/4$ cup of lightly salted water to a boil. Add the corn and fava beans or peas and simmer for 3 minutes. Add the butter and tomatoes and sauté for another 2 minutes, stirring frequently, until the vegetables become tender. Season with salt and pepper. Add the basil and chives just before serving. Garnish with the basil sprigs.

Overnight Pickles

Makes about 1½ cups

6 Kirby cucumbers, cut into $1/8$-inch slices

$1/2$ cup white wine vinegar

$1/2$ cup sugar

1 teaspoon salt

5 fresh dill or tarragon sprigs

Place the cucumbers in a large pickling jar. In a large bowl, mix all of the ingredients with 4 cups of water, making sure the sugar and salt are completely dissolved. Pour the mixture into the jar with the pickles. Refrigerate it for up to a week.

Potatoes

POTATOES SEEM LIKE SUCH AN UNCOMPLICATED FOOD, SIMPLE TO INTERPRET, EASY TO UNDERSTAND. But there is so much more to understanding and making great potatoes than managing to find some at the grocery store that aren't so old they've grown eyes.

Potatoes are Maine's largest agricultural crop. Potato farming actually takes place on the western side of the Northern Woods, in Aroostook County, where potatoes are a way of life. Each September when the crops are ready, everyone puts their daily activities on hold to help with the harvest. Even schoolchildren work the fields and get paid by the bucket.

Shoestring Fries

Serves 4

3 large Idaho potatoes, peeled
1 quart peanut oil (canola or vegetable is fine)
Kosher salt

At Pearl we use a mandoline to cut the fries. If you happen to have one, it certainly helps the job go faster and you will have a more consistent size. If you're doing this by hand, slice the potatoes into 1/16-inch slices, then stack the slices and julienne them into thin strips. Place them in the refrigerator in a bowl of cold water half an hour before frying. This will leach out some of the starch and the potatoes will fry better.

Drain the potatoes in a colander until they are dry.

In a deep-fat fryer, heat the oil to 350°F. If you don't have a thermometer, drop in a piece of potato and make sure it rises quickly to the surface. In small batches, drop the fries carefully into the oil in one layer—don't crowd them. Blanch them for about 2 minutes and pull them out with a slotted spoon.

Place them on a cookie sheet to await the second fry. When all the potatoes have had a first fry, put them back in the oil in small batches and fry them until they are golden brown, about 2 minutes. Drain the fries on paper towels and salt them immediately. Serve them with *anything!*

Potato Tart

Serves 4

3 Idaho potatoes, peeled
4 tablespoons clarified butter (page 62) or olive oil
8 medium shiitake mushrooms, stems removed, and julienned
Leaves from 4 or 5 thyme sprigs
Kosher salt and freshly ground black pepper

With a mandoline or by hand, slice the potatoes into $1/16$-inch disks. Place them in the refrigerator in a bowl of cold water. Heat an ovenproof 10-inch skillet over medium heat, add 2 tablespoons of the butter and the mushrooms, and sauté the mushrooms until light brown, about 3 to 4 minutes. Stir in the thyme. Set the mushrooms aside in a small bowl.

Drain the potatoes in a colander until dry.

Preheat the oven to 475°F. Rinse the pan and wipe it out. Heat the pan over medium heat and add the remaining 2 tablespoons of butter. In the pan over low heat, put a layer of potato slices in circles that spiral out to the edge of the pan. Season with salt and pepper. Place a second layer of potatoes the same way and season it. Add the mushrooms, spreading them evenly around the tart. Add another potato layer and continue until all the potatoes are used, lightly seasoning each layer.

Bake the tart for about 12 minutes. Check the underside by lifting the edge with a spatula to see if it's golden brown. If it's not ready, return it to the oven for a few more minutes. Now comes the hard part. Slide a large spatula under the tart and carefully flip it. Bake until the other side is golden brown, about 12 minutes. Set on paper towels to drain. Cut into quarters and serve.

Potato Pancakes

Serves 4 to 6

I like to serve these with soft, poached eggs for breakfast or with smoked salmon and crème fraîche and caviar.

3 medium Idaho potatoes, peeled and grated
1 medium onion, grated
2 eggs
$1/4$ cup flour
Kosher salt and freshly ground black pepper
$1/2$ cup clarified butter (page 62)

Preheat the oven to 400°F. Squeeze some of the liquid from the potatoes and onion either in a paper towel or by hand. In a large bowl, mix together the potatoes, onion, eggs, and flour. Add salt and pepper to taste. Form the mixture into small patties about 2 inches in diameter and $1/2$ inch thick. Try to leave the edges a little rough because they'll look rather pretty and lacy when fried. In a 10-inch skillet over medium heat, melt the clarified butter and add some of the pancakes (don't crowd the pan). You may want to use two pans at once because the potato mixture browns as it's exposed to the air, so you'll want to work quickly. Cook the pancakes until they are golden brown on the bottom, about 3 to 4 minutes, then flip them and brown the other side for 3 to 4 more minutes. Remove them from the pan and drain on paper towels. Place on an ovenproof cookie sheet or dish and finish them in the oven for 5 minutes. To find out if they're cooked, try one of the pancakes—the center should be creamy and cooked through.

A Summer Table

My mother and her cousins Marc, Ted, and George were city kids used to cement playgrounds and screeching cars. But each August they ran free, surrounded by clean water, green grass, and fresh air. They played tag in the tree groves, pinched an occasional tomato from the garden, and experimented with lawn games such as croquet and badminton when the adults weren't monopolizing them.

One of my mother's favorite things was jumping down from the old hayloft in the barn into the huge pillows of hay below. (When I was little and we stayed at Forest Hill, she would point out the exact spot, showing me how high the hay was piled.) Ellie loved having her cousins to play with, and they were endlessly fascinated by watching the cows get milked and seeing eggs collected from the chickens. Like many of the small hotels throughout New England at the time, most of the vegetables and dairy products came from the hotel's farm. The dining room served only Forest Hill guests, but could seat one hundred (in the early days) at tables of eight and four. Every night throughout the summer, families had the same table and the same waitress.

La Rosa Pedro Maria Captivilla Daniels, a light-skinned black woman,

From the bottom up, Ted, Ellie and Marc at the Forest Hill House, circa 1929.

cooked at the Forest Hill House from the early 1920s through the late 1940s. Dorothy remembers Rosa as a dedicated and talented cook who counted among her little quirks wearing a starched white nurse's cap over her hair while she cooked. Everyone became quite attached to Rosa, who hand-tatted handkerchiefs as gifts each Christmas. My mother remembers Rosa well and says she was always kind to the kids, giving out extra cookies or letting them help in the kitchen when they seemed bored or it was raining. Mostly, Mom remembers what she describes as "incredible home cooking."

As was the custom of that time, a hearty breakfast was served in the morning with the largest meal of the day, dinner, served between noon and one, followed by a lighter supper between six and seven. From eight until nine each morning, he-man, Maine logger breakfasts of steak, liver and onions, eggs cooked to order, bacon, and pancakes with Maine maple syrup were served, always with hand-squeezed orange juice.

After breakfast, everyone would go his or her own way. Fifteen or twenty minutes before dinner (also before supper) one of the waitresses would go outside and ring a loud bell to call everyone to the dining room. Dorothy hated that job. "This wasn't a little service bell, it was a big loud ship's bell that clanged when you slung it back and forth. To feed that many people you really had to keep to a schedule, and if guests were more than fifteen minutes late for a meal, they were frowned upon by the help."

Rosa focused many of her efforts on traditional Maine and New England fare, which included lots of fish, shellfish, chowders, and fish stews. There were meats such as turkey or lamb, plain baked potatoes or rich, scalloped potatoes made with fresh cream from the cows, breads still warm from the oven, and bowls of vegetables just out of the garden. At six in the evening supper was usually cold or room-temperature meat with cold salads, or fish stews. My mom loved the nights when they served diver's scallops that were succulent and shimmering like giant sea pearls, broiled plain with a little butter and a sprinkle of bread crumbs. Usually within a few days of the Goldsmiths' arrival, the sweet corn was ready for picking, and my mom says they crunched their way through the rest of the summer with butter and salt dripping down their chins. At the end of every meal was an array of desserts, including pies, cakes, and puddings.

My family really looked forward to the weekends, when their hosts threw Friday evening clambakes in a special pit dug in the hotel's side yard and Sunday afternoon shore dinners with enormous pots of fresh lobsters cooking over the fire. David Toothaker and Rosa presided over the cooking of these events, checking the seaweed covered pit of the clambake or making sure the corn and lobsters didn't get overcooked for the shore dinner.

Rosa left Forest Hill sometime in the late 1940s and retired to a small two-room apartment in New York City, where Dorothy and May visited her a few times. May and her husband ran the Forest Hill House until the early 1970s, when they sold it to the first of a series of owners who let it fall into increasing disrepair. Blue shag carpeting covered the old wood floors and *mod* 1970s wallpaper found its way onto many of the walls. Fortunately, it was bought by someone who saw its potential and given a renaissance in the 1980s. The White Barn Inn, as it is now called, was restored to its former glory, and then turned into an upscale New England inn, complete with a flagstone pool.

Scallops

SCALLOPS CAN BE A LITTLE DAUNTING FOR THE AT-HOME COOK, ESPECIALLY IF YOU ARE TRYING TO DUPLICATE WHAT YOU ORDER IN A RESTAURANT. After all, the old days of soaking little mushy disks of scallop flesh in butter and cooking them until they are like marbles is a thing of the past (remnants of our moms). Actually, cooking scallops at home is quick and easy, but you have to learn a little technique. Remember, the two things you need to make good scallops are a good product and high heat.

Deep Sea or Bay Scallops?

(See also Wet vs. Dry Scallops, page 13.)

The answer really depends on your taste. Because of their origins, I am partial to deep-sea scallops, which are taken from the bottom of the cold Atlantic off the coast of Maine and up into Nova Scotia. Sometimes called ocean or Maine diver scallops, they are large and firm and perfect for sautéing. One of my greatest joys is to order Maine diver scallops when I go out. (Although I cook them every day at Pearl, I seldom get the chance to eat them.) I also use them in scallop chowder, pan roasts, and my scallop casserole, because they are nice, big, and meaty. I feel like I get more value with them. Frankly, they are just easier to cook on the stove and less time-consuming. But bay scallops also from the Atlantic are often sweeter than the deep-sea scallop. They are impossible to sauté, however, because they are so small. They are best broiled or used in dishes where it's harder to overcook them. They are also delicious raw.

Pan-Seared Scallops

Serves 2

I like to serve scallops on a bed of risotto in the winter or on a vegetable ragout in the summer—especially on the Sweet Corn Ragout (page 69). Anything with tomatoes compliments the sweetness of scallops perfectly, and they are also lovely with roasted vegetables and bacon. When I was cooking in the early 1990s, I served my version of a BLT in which I put caramelized scallops on a bacon and potato tart with tomato butter sauce.

4 scallops per person, U-10 size (10 per pound)
Kosher salt and freshly ground black pepper
Peanut or vegetable oil for sautéing

Cooking scallops can be difficult at home because it is hard to get a pan as hot on your home stove as we can get it on a restaurant stove. Some of the newer model stoves, however, are now being made with one burner that has a higher BTU output, so eventually home cooks will be able to prepare seared foods in the same way a restaurant does.

Season the scallops lightly on both sides with salt and pepper. Put your pan on very high heat. Do *not* add the oil until you're certain the pan is hot. When you add the oil it should shimmer and you might see wisps of smoke— too much smoke means the pan is too hot. Immediately put your scallops in the pan, flat side down. After 2 minutes, lift the edges gently. When the scallops are caramelized and a mahogany brown color, turn them over and reduce the heat by half. When they are firm to the touch, which should take another minute or two, they're done. Serve them immediately, as scallops tend to lose their juice once they're cooked.

Scalloped Scallops

Serves 4 as an appetizer

According to the French, anything baked in a scallop shell is escalloped. This dish is reminiscent of something my mom, and I'm certain moms across the country, made in the 1960s, after Julia Child came into all our kitchens. It's a take on what was called coquilles St. Jacques. It can be served as a first course, or a larger portion can be served as an entrée.

I love truffle butter and use it in this recipe. If it's available in your area, buy it and keep it in the refrigerator, because it can be used to enhance almost anything, from scrambled eggs to chicken. It's particularly good in dishes with mushrooms, and finishes gravies and sauces beautifully.

Scallop shells can be purchased in certain gourmet food stores. Or, if you're lucky enough to have a fishmonger who can get scallops live in the shell, clean the shells and save them for use as a serving dish.

3 medium shallots, chopped

2 tablespoons ($1/4$ stick) unsalted butter

Kosher salt

8 medium white mushrooms, chopped

$1/2$ cup amontillado sherry

$1^1/3$ cups heavy cream

Freshly ground black pepper

8 medium to large sea scallops

2 tablespoons cooking oil

4 scallop shells, for presentation

$1/2$ cup bread crumbs

1 tablespoon truffle butter (optional)

1 tablespoon finely chopped chervil or flat-leaf parsley

In a medium saucepan, over low heat, sauté the shallots in 1 tablespoon of butter, seasoned with a small pinch of salt, until they are softened but without color, about 5 to 8 minutes. Place them in a bowl. Add another tablespoon of butter to the pan and sauté the mushrooms seasoned with a small pinch of salt about 4 to 5 minutes, or until they are lightly browned. Return the shallots to the pan and deglaze with the sherry. Reduce the liquid to about a tablespoon. Add the heavy cream and reduce it by half. Season to taste with salt and pepper and keep it warm on the back of the stove until ready to use.

Preheat the oven to 425°F. Season the scallops lightly on both sides with salt and pepper. Heat a 10-inch skillet over high heat and add the cooking oil. Just before the oil heats to the smoking point, lay the scallops in the pan on their flat side and sear them until they're caramelized, about 3 minutes. Turn them over and turn off the heat.

Place the scallop shells on a cookie sheet and arrange 2 scallops in each shell. Spoon the sauce around the scallops (try not to cover the caramelized top), sprinkle it with bread crumbs, and dot it with truffle butter, if using. Bake the scallops for about 5 minutes, until the bread crumbs are browned. Garnish with the chervil. Serve immediately on plates with doilies so that the shells don't slip.

Taylor Bay Scallops in the Shell with Leeks and Butter Sauce

Serves 2

1 small leek

1 cup white wine

Kosher salt and freshly ground black pepper

16 Nantucket or Taylor Bay scallops in the shell

$1/2$ pound unsalted cold butter, cut into small pieces

Prepare the leek by trimming off the dark green top and roots, slicing the white part in half lengthwise, and cutting it into $\frac{1}{4}$-inch slices. Immerse the leek slices in a bowl of cold water and agitate them to loosen and remove the sand. Skim the leeks out of the water and into a strainer, leaving the sand behind.

In a large saucepan over medium heat, bring the wine to a simmer. Add the leeks and a small pinch of salt and sauté for about 2 minutes. Add the scallops in the shell and cover the pan tightly. Raise the heat and steam until the shells open, about 3 to 4 minutes. Check them halfway through to make sure there is still liquid in the pan. If not, add more wine or water. When the shells open, leave the leeks in the pan but remove the scallops. Place them in a bowl in a warm place while you make the sauce.

To prepare the simple pan butter sauce, over medium-high heat, reduce the liquid in the pan to about 1 tablespoon. Add the chunks of cold butter, whisking constantly. Work quickly, or the sauce will break. Once all the butter has been incorporated, pull it off the heat and season it to taste. Pour the sauce over the scallops and serve.

The Darling of the Gods

"AUGUST IS THE DARLING OF THE GODS. Month of fun and frolic, love and laughter, play and pleasure," wrote *The Wave* in August 1910. I can't say I'm much of a frolicker, even in Maine, but there is something particularly special about being in Kennebunkport during August. For decades popular wisdom held that if you were traveling to Paris, never go in August because the city shuts down for vacation. New York seems to be taking a page from that travel book, seemingly empty except for a few determined souls who insist on seeing the city despite the scorching heat and a few natives who believe in air conditioning as a religion and honestly enjoy having the city to themselves. Even city kids with entry-level jobs pool their minimal resources to rent a house

Ellie on Independence Day, circa 1928.

in Long Island or in New Jersey, as near to the beach as their expenses will allow. There they sleep four to a room every other weekend just to be somewhere other than the city. I know how they feel. For me, cooking in a steamy kitchen on sweltering hot days lost its charm a long time ago. As Pearl Oyster Bar's annual summer vacation approaches, all I can think about is sitting on Gooch's Beach.

The Husband Express

When August came around, my grandmother was thrilled to get out of the city for four or five weeks. Chasing a toddler around a hot Manhattan apartment in the middle of a heat wave could not have been very pleasant. With no air conditioning, she had a family to feed three times a day. A ninety-degree apartment seldom inspires the kind of culinary reverie that brings creativity to the dinner table. In that heat, you don't even want to throw a roast or a chicken in the oven for two hours. You probably don't even want to flip on the gas to cook vegetables or boil an egg. By late July, there were pretty much no such things as cold dinners, because while Electrolux had sold their one-millionth refrigerator by 1936, in 1924 families still had iceboxes. The best Pearle could hope for was a dinner marginally cooler than room temperature. Since she couldn't keep much fresh in the summer heat, even in an icebox, it meant walking the sultry streets daily, strolling a toddler in a pram to buy fresh food. By the time they hit the roads to Maine, my grandmother was longing for the cool sea breezes and the crisp ocean spray.

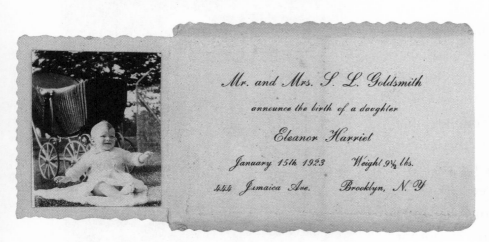

Mr. and Mrs. S. L. Goldsmith
announce the birth of a daughter
Eleanor Harriet
January 15th 1923   Weight 9½ lbs.
444 Jamaica Ave.   Brooklyn, N. Y.

For my grandfather, who loved the seashore and went to Coney Island when he was young, spending time in Maine was somewhat more complex. Goldie would drive Pearle and Eleanor up, stay for the weekend, and then take the train back to New York so that he could be at work Monday morning. On Friday or Thursday evening he was back on the train bound for the seashore, New York to Boston, Boston to Kennebunkport. Those hot train rides back and forth were a sort of *husband express,* filled with men from New

York and Boston going to meet their families on the Cape, Nantucket, Martha's Vineyard, or the southern coast of Maine. At the end of the summer, Goldie would take his two or three weeks of vacation and, with great relief, go up to Maine to stay.

Spouting Rock and Blowing Cave

For both my family and my great-uncle's family, the water and the seashore lifestyle was captivating. Perhaps the best thing about the Forest Hill House was that the Atlantic Ocean was a two-minute walk down the road: close enough to smell the sea air at the hotel and hear the tide at night through the open windows. Pearle and little Eleanor spent long days walking from one end of Gooch's Beach to the other and almost always ventured as far onto the breakwater as they could. For a long time my mother said she wanted her ashes launched from those rocks when the time came.

People sit and fish from the breakwater, or test their coordination by walking all the way to the end. If it starts to rain once you're out there, I don't think it's too dramatic to say that you are in for the scariest walk back of your life. When I lived in Kennebunk, the very end of the breakwater became the spot where I would go to sit and think. A couple of times a week, I would bring a bottle of wine out there, watch the sunset, and try to figure out what the hell was going to happen to me and where my life would take me. When it was time to return to

Goldie and Ellie on the 4th of July, 1928.

shore, I'd run back over the rocks, which varied in height and size and made this a dangerous, crazy obstacle course, especially after a bottle of wine. In recent years, I've occasionally been tempted to try it while I'm out there, but almost twenty years later, I know better.

From there you get a terrific view of the ivy-covered St. Ann's Episcopal Church, which was made from stones plucked from the bottom of the ocean. Set on a little green that extends out into the water, it is the epitome of serene and has incredible views too, including Walker's Point. But the most magnificent view comes when you look right down the beach.

The three Kennebunk beaches, forming a scalloped edge on the coast, offer the best of the Maine coastline. We go to Gooch's Beach, a wide, flat expanse of white sand that of the trio of beaches is the nicest for bathing. The dunes are small but protect the beach from the wind, and there are no rocks until the breakwater. The Atlantic rolls in great, frothy crests that can knock you off your feet with their strength. In the past few years, would-be surfers have tried to ride these waves, but they end up spending most of their time sitting on their boards, bobbing up and down like buoys. Middle Beach comes next, beginning at the tidal pools across the street from what once was the Narragansett Hotel and is now the Narragansett Condominiums. The rocky shoreline looks like it belongs farther Down East and is a great walking beach for anyone wearing shoes. Then there's Mother's Beach, perfect for small kids because it's tucked into a sheltered cove; with waves that are no more than ripples, it's as gentle as a pond.

Together, our families have put in countless miles walking those beaches. My mother still walks all the way from the breakwater to the tidal pools and back each day she's there. It's sort of an unwritten rule in my family that once you start, you have to go from one end to the other and back. I still feel like a slacker if I don't see the walk through, regardless of how hot, cold, or wet the weather may be.

If it's hot, as it generally is through August, you may actually be so warm that you need a dip in the Atlantic to cool off. It is *always* shocking to me how cold that water is. I've been in it in May, and I've been in it in August. The only real difference I've ever noticed is that the cold just feels better when you're melting from the heat. More to the point, I am a member of the *Jaws* generation, so I rarely go out over my knees anyway—you just don't know what's out there.

My grandmother loved the water and to swim, although I still wonder if she learned to swim in America, England, or Scotland. The Forest Hill House had an arrangement with a lovely private bathhouse on Gooch's Beach (the only one still standing today), which allowed guests to have their own lockers.

My mom in 1927— Shirley Temple, eat your heart out.

My grandmother would take my mother's hand and they'd walk roughly half a mile from the hotel to the beach, dressed in their summer clothes: pressed, pleated skirts and crisp white shirts for my grandmother, and puff-sleeved, Empire-waist organdy dresses for my mother. Once there, they'd change into their bathing costumes at the long white beach house, which had rows of identical little doors going from one end to the other that led out onto a beautiful, privately owned section of Gooch's Beach. The rooms were tiny and had a built-in bench in the corner and enough room to store your beach chairs and umbrella overnight, and for an adult and child to change at the same time. Pearle would hang their clothes on the hooks, leave the beach picnic Rosa had packed for them on the little bench where it would stay cool until lunch, take their umbrella, and head out to the beach.

There are some great pictures of my mom playing on Gooch's Beach when she was a little girl, and there's something comforting about seeing your parent as a happy child. My grandmother dressed her in wonderful bathing suits that had belts at the waist and legs that went almost to the knee. She always wore beach hats or caps that made her look as if she stepped out of an early *Our Gang* episode.

Ellie, Marc, Ted, and Minna's son, George, would play long, exhausting games of hide-and-seek in the tall beach grass, which was, and still is, so high and thick that any number of children could move through it for hours and never get found. Each summer they started new collections of seashells, sand dollars, and starfish, with the cousins constantly trying to outdo one another. They built sand castles and played pirates, forming alliances that shifted with the tide. They would watch as prep school kids from Boston played impromptu cricket games in the sand or played catch with their lacrosse sticks.

By three o'clock when the sea breeze would blow in and make it too cold to stay down there, they would shower off the sand under one of the bathhouse's outdoor showers, get dressed, and bring their beach clothes and towels back to the hotel to dry overnight. Uninitiated guests who left their things at the beach house got quite a shock—their things would be just as wet as they had left them. (Hotel bed sheets and towels had to be washed and dried by the time the sea breeze rolled in too, or they would never dry.)

Beach houses served an important function before World War II, because polite people did not appear in bathing clothes anywhere but on the beach. At the turn of the century Kennebunk beaches were lined with private bathing houses, but by the end of World War I few were left standing. Instead they built public beach houses that offered lots of services. Sometimes as a special treat, one of the adults would take the kids to a nearby public bathing house where they could get a cold drink to have with their lunch or some ice cream. Perhaps the most celebrated of the Kennebunks' public bathing houses was the Dipsy Bathing Pavilion, which was built on Seashore Company land by William O. Littlefield. The Dipsy baths could be seen from well up the road and out into the water because of the beautiful display created by its enormous signature brown-and-white-striped beach umbrellas. A marvel of variety, you could do everything at Dipsy from shower and change, to play billiards, to patronize the barber shop or steam laundry. Ice creams and other sweets were for sale, as well as imported Cuban cigars, magazines, fishing tackle, stationery, bathing clothes, sodas, lemonades, and other temperance drinks. In addition to the changing rooms and showers, there were separate sun parlors where men and women could sit politely and take the sun, hot salt baths, and afternoon tea at the Daisy Shop. These bathhouses were more than just a sunny-day attraction. With all of these activities available, they were meant to keep the beach fun, even when it rained.

Ellie ready for the beach from head to toe, circa 1929.

On the walk back from the bathhouse, the smells of cigar smoke, strawberry ice cream, and sea air all mingled together. Uncle Sam and my grandfather, who usually took the kids on the long walk so that the women wouldn't have to change back to their street clothes, smoked their cigars while the kids ate their ice cream cones. Often the group would stop to watch prep-school boys playing lacrosse or rugby games. Then, back at their towels, they would head to the water. Pearle swam in the ocean most days, and even when I was a young girl, I remember her little round figure done up in a flowered bathing suit headed out toward the waves, a little white cap perched on her gray hair.

Canoes were still very important, although the utter dominance of power-boats, prompted by Prohibition and rum-running, was about to take hold.

Goldie down front and Pearle, getting a leg up, behind him with the help of brothers-in-law Lew (left) and Ben (right). This may have been pre– or post–tennis game at Forest Hill.

There were weekly races on the river and annual regattas. Couples would paddle over to Picnic Rock, a large hunk of granite that hung out into the river. They'd bring their picnics and spend long, romantic hours there. Sometimes entire families would come to picnic or have more elegant evening parties with paper lanterns, chafing dishes filled with lobster Newburg, and bottles of champagne tucked away under the blankets. In the 1920s, strains of ukulele music would occasionally be heard coming down from the pines. Although my grandparents never did frequent Picnic Rock, my aunt and uncle did punt over there several times. Some afternoons my family would all drive out to Ocean Avenue, toward Walker's Point, to see Spouting Rock and Blowing Cave. When the tides are just right, the water comes in and shoots spectacularly up and over the rocks in a tremendous glittering shower.

The big event each August, as it had been since 1885, was the annual carnival, sponsored by the Lobster Boat and Canoe Club. Some years more than three hundred boats, including canoes, dories, fishing boats, and small yachts, would join in, each one strung from bow to stern with brightly colored Chinese lanterns that would be lit as the pageant began. Participating boats would gather at the boathouse that evening, at a time determined by when the tide was right, falling in behind one another as they took off, sailing majestically down the Kennebunk River. At the mouth of the Atlantic the procession blossomed, fanning out slightly, and gliding into the complete blackness of the ocean and sky. Private cottages, hotels, and other businesses would decorate their areas by stringing lanterns around their yards, porches, picket fences, and anything else that would hold them. For those watching from land or sea, it was a dazzling sight.

Fish Tails

When the Goldsmith men and boys came up, they liked to try their hand with a reel and rod, so several times during the vacation, my grandfather, Uncle Sam, and the boys would set off for the Kennebunk River early in the morning. They dressed for a day on the water, carrying flasks of lemonade and water and a hefty fisherman's lunch that Rosa packed for them. In that lunch pail (literally a clam bucket with a few layers of printed cotton napkins thrown over it) would be thick sandwiches made from chicken salad, or whatever roasted meats were left over from the last day's menu, on slices of Rosa's freshly baked pullman loaf, wrapped in paper napkins. Sometimes there was a jar of homemade pickles or pickled beets; other times there were bowls of potato salad. There was always something sweet, either half a layer cake iced with just a dusting of powdered sugar so it would be easy to eat or a fresh double-crust fruit pie, already cut into sixths.

Sometimes the boys would sit on the banks of the river, their lines dangling into the water, talking and joking, occasionally catching a slim, silvery trout, smallmouth bass, or a prized salmon. Other times, like serious fishermen out for a day of adventure, they rented a canoe from one of the Indians or a small dory down at the town docks. Fishing guides were popular in the area and sometimes Uncle Sam enlisted their help. The Native American guides had been fishing in these waters for centuries and knew where the fish were every time, although there weren't as many of them and they weren't as interested in working as guides by the mid-1920s. In town, elderly fishermen and sea captains who didn't work commercially anymore but still wanted to be on the water making a little money offered their services. They knew about casting a line and the intricacies of tying flies and baiting a hook. If Native Americans had an ancient spiritual bond with these waters, naming them and living on them before the white man, then the expertise of local fishing guides came from nearly three hundred years spent getting to know these waters well enough to make a successful living from them.

Between the two cultures, the gang (which sometimes included Pearle's brothers), who had spent their whole lives in big cities, learned to love fishing. In the evening, they would bring their fish, gutted, cleaned, and strung on a line, to the Forest Hill House, where Rosa would cook them up for them. That night the Goldsmiths would have the freshest fish imaginable, hours out of the Kennebunk River, dusted with flour and fried lightly in butter and oil until slightly crisp on the edges and tender on the inside. Served with a few slices of lemon, it was a wonderful feast but in truth . . . it was rather rare. Those city boys were not great fishermen, but they always had fun.

So much of August in the Kennebunks revolved around the water for my family. Even when it rained you went to the beach for long walks and entertained yourselves at the bathing houses. But there was plenty for families to do in town, too, and the entire month was filled with afternoon dances and visits to Dock Square. They listened to band concerts in the square and looked in the gift shops. My grandmother, an inveterate knitter, liked to visit the Little Gray Shoppe of Newport, Rhode Island, and Kennebunkport and look through their array of yarns. Later, of course, she would sit on the beach in the hot August sun, knitting away at some piece of winter clothing for the next year. By the end of each August, everybody in the Chicago contingent went home with a new scarf knitted by Aunt Beck.

Every year there was a country fair with Punch and Judy shows, colorful dancing girls, and what the Kennebunk *Star* in August 1924 called "a costly

menagerie" of wild animals. There were hot dogs and peanuts and tables covered with sweets like rich red velvet cakes with snow white icing, carrot cakes
thick with cream cheese frosting, giant five-layer devil's food cakes, big
squares of spicy gingerbread, and coconut cakes covered in a flurry of toasted
coconut. There were circus clowns and a gypsy fortune-teller billed as "the seventh daughter of a seventh son," and stalls with delicate needlework and
other "fancy work" made by local women. But my grandmother's favorite pastime in the Kennebunks had nothing to do with the beach and everything to
do with food.

Fillet Fish

FISH . . . FEEL THE FEAR AND COOK IT ANYWAY. Once you learn how to pick out and cook fish, you will find that there is *nothing* quicker, easier, and healthier to cook. Some dishes like bouillabaisse, chowders, and stews take longer to make, so perhaps it's better to save those for the weekend when you have more prep time. But a fillet of fish takes almost no time at all and makes a perfect, quick weeknight dinner.

Fish Buying Tips

I would never buy fish prewrapped in a supermarket. If your market has an open-air fish stall where the fish is displayed on ice, that's ideal. Ask the fishmonger to hold it out for you to smell. I know this is difficult in most stores now because the counters are very high and the employees may act put out by the extra effort. But do it anyway. Your guests will thank you for it. Back when most of our grandparents were young and purchasing things at market, they wouldn't have brought home so much as a tomato without sticking their nose in it. The fish should have no smell or, if anything, a faint smell of the sea. Cloudy eyes and brown gills mean that the fish has been dead for way too long.

When you are buying from the loin, buy the center cut. Pieces from the tail end are often sinewy. Pieces from the head end of a large loin can be so wide that to get the right portion size you would have to cut them too thin.

Ask for the fish to be cut in a one-piece chunk big enough for 1 to $1^1/_2$ inches in length per person. Then portion it yourself at home. This is especially important if you're not using it that day because the fish will stay fresher this way.

Pan-Roasted Salmon

Serves 2

The art of cooking fish is not about a long list of ingredients—it's about getting the freshest possible product and learning to cook well. Many people serve salmon on the rare side, but I don't care for that. I think that the salmon's flavor is much richer when the oil in the fish is fully cooked. This is not to say I like it dry, so paying attention to cooking time is very important with salmon. Served with vegetables or salad, this is one of the healthiest and most convenient dishes you can feed yourself and your family for dinner.

1 tablespoon peanut, canola, or olive oil

Kosher salt and freshly ground black pepper

2 7- to 8-ounce salmon fillets, skin removed

Preheat the oven to 450°F. Using an ovenproof sauté pan, add the oil over high heat, and let it heat until just before the smoking point. Season both sides of the fillets, then lay them carefully in the pan, presentation-side down. (The presentation side is the side that was closest to the bone and did not have the skin on it.) If the pan seems too hot at this point, turn the heat down a bit. Give the pan a little shake to make sure the fillets don't stick. If they do stick, don't try to unstick them in the beginning—wait until the fish develops a little crust and you'll find it's much easier to get the fish off the pan. The fillets will take about 3 minutes to attain a nice golden color. Flip the fish and finish it in the oven, about 4 to 5 minutes.

You can use this same method of cooking for snapper and sea bass fillets. Wild striped bass is generally served with the skin on, and skin-on fillets are generally cooked with the skin side down in a small amount of oil. As soon as the skin begins to get a little crispy, finish it in the oven for 5 to 6 minutes, or until the bass looks pure white, with no translucency. To serve, flip it over so the skin side faces up for presentation. If you want to leave the skin on for the salmon, use this method.

Pan-Roasted Cod

Serves 2

Fish like cod, haddock, flounder, and sole are traditionally cooked as skinless fillets and floured, giving them a nice golden crust. I prefer to use a mixture of flour and cracker meal for a more interesting texture.

This method of cooking does require a little more oil to cook, because you do want a little browning on the sides of the fish.

2 6- to 7-ounce cod, haddock, flounder, or sole fillets

1 cup milk

Kosher salt and freshly ground black pepper

$^2/_3$ cup flour

$^1/_3$ cup cracker meal

$^1/_4$ cup canola, peanut, or soy oil

Preheat the oven to 450°F. Soak the fillets in milk for 5 minutes before cooking to give the fish a little sweetness and remove any unpleasant fishy flavor. Remove the fish from the milk, lay it on a plate, and season it with salt and pepper. On a large plate, combine the flour and cracker meal. Dredge the fish on both sides in the flour mixture, coating it thoroughly. Pat off any excess. In an ovenproof 10-inch pan over high heat, add the oil and heat it to just below the smoking point.

Place the fillets in the pan, presentation-side down. Lower the heat to medium. When the crust is golden brown, about 3 to 4 minutes, flip the fillets over and finish them in the oven for about 4 to 5 minutes. When the fish is done, you will see traces of albumen (the white protein the fish exudes) appearing in the cracks of the crust. This is your telltale thermometer.

Flat fish like flounder or sole cook more quickly; 2 to 3 minutes in the oven should finish them.

Pan Roasted Skate with Brussels Sprouts and Bacon

Serves 2

2 medium skate wings, filleted

1 cup milk

$^1/_3$ cup cracker meal

$^2/_3$ cup flour

Kosher salt and freshly ground black pepper

$^1/_4$ cup canola or peanut oil

Brussel Sprouts and Bacon (recipe follows)

4 lemon wedges

Preheat oven to 450°F. Soak the fillets in a dish of milk for 5 minutes, then drain and lay on a plate. On a large plate or in a shallow bowl, combine the cracker meal and flour. Season both sides of the fillets with salt and pepper and then dredge in the mixture, coating thoroughly. Pat off any excess. In an ovenproof pan over high heat, add the oil and heat to just below the smoking point.

Place the fillets in the pan, presentation side down. Lower the heat to medium. When the crust is golden brown, about 3 to 4 minutes, flip the fillets over and finish them in the oven for about 4 to 5 minutes. When the fish is done, the natural striations of the fish will flake apart easily.

To serve, mound the vegetables at 12 o'clock on the plate and place the skate fillet underneath them. Garnish each plate with 2 lemon wedges.

Brussels Sprouts and Bacon

2 tablespoons of $1/4$-inch-diced raw bacon

1 shallot, chopped

1 small clove of garlic, finely chopped

1 small carrot, diced

12 brussels sprouts, cut into quarters

2 tablespoons unsalted butter

Kosher salt and freshly ground black pepper

1 teaspoon chopped flat-leaf parsley

In an 8-inch sauté pan, render the bacon over medium heat, cooking until the bacon starts to brown. Add the shallot and the garlic and sauté until they are translucent. Add the carrot and the brussels sprouts and mix thoroughly. Add $1/2$ cup of water and cover. Steam the vegetables for 3 to 4 minutes, or until they are tender. Remove the cover and you should have about 1 tablespoon of liquid left in the pan. If not, add a little. Finish with 2 tablespoons of butter, tossing constantly until the butter is incorporated. Add salt and pepper to taste and the parsley, tossing a few more times.

Fried Cod Sandwich

Serves 2

This is an old New England sandwich that can also be made with haddock or, for a more Southern flavor, grouper. Having lived in Maine, I am used to eating this sandwich on a soft roll, but I have come to prefer it on a hard, crusty roll. It really does change the entire sandwich. At Pearl, we use ciabatta from Sullivan Street Bakery.

2 ciabatta rolls

$1/4$ to $1/2$ cup Pearl Oyster Bar Tartar Sauce (page 157)

$1/2$ tomato, thinly sliced

$1/2$ red onion, thinly sliced

4 to 6 Bibb or Boston lettuce leaves

Kosher salt and freshly ground black pepper

2 pan-roasted cod fillets (page 94)

Toast the rolls in the oven for 1 or 2 minutes. Slice them lengthwise with a sharp, serrated knife and spread each side liberally with tartar sauce. On the bottom half, layer the tomato, onion, and greens and lightly season to taste with salt and pepper. Put the fillet on top and close the sandwich.

Low Tea at High Tide

WE NEVER DRANK A LOT OF COFFEE IN MY FAMILY. Probably from years spent growing up in the United Kingdom, my grandmother would rather have had a cup of tea over coffee anytime. My mother and I inherited this preference from Pearle, much the way we inherited our bad backs, love of cats and cocktails, and Puritan work ethic. My mother has a cup of coffee but not until after she has had a cup of tea, and I know my day is off to a questionable start when I only have time for one cup. Coffee is fine. I certainly drink enough of it while I'm at work where, on a busy night, I'll have to shuck two to three hundred oysters and cook for 250 people. But there is something refined about leisurely drinking a warm cup of tea. It just seems like a gentler way to start your day, regardless of whether you are a purist who buys the finest blends of tea leaves or someone like me who is happy with a Twining's tea bag.

My mother and grandmother sitting on the rocks between Gooch's and Middle Beaches, circa 1927.

While it doesn't happen with every single cup, tea is something that often makes me think of my grandmother. I'd give almost anything to sit down with her over a pot of tea and be able to ask her questions about everything from her childhood, to performing at the Metropolitan and City operas, to my grandfather and their summers in Kennebunkport.

For my grandmother, a tearoom was more than a social event, it was a nostalgic trip back to her childhood in Glasgow, where she spent many of her happiest days. The first tearooms had sprung up in 1875, and they soon became an integral part of society and the city's business community. As a young girl, Pearle would often take afternoon tea in these little shops, and it was a tradition she was happy to see cross the Atlantic. In America, tea service had originally become a social event in the late 1880s, at posh hotels like the Ritz and the Plaza. Catering to a wealthy clientele, these elegant hotel tearooms embodied genteel living, with their silver tea services and chamber music.

Storefront tearooms, or tea salons, which brought tea service to popular culture, didn't become prevalent until after the turn of the century. Resort areas took to the craze and by the 1920s, New England towns especially had become known for their tearooms. They provided a great place for women to socialize in the summer afternoons, while the men were back in the city working and children were off playing by the water. Tearooms in resorts were more egalitarian than their hotel counterparts, and the same room might easily draw a society matron holding a private tea as well as middle-class sightseers who had come to sit and rest.

Tearooms were run exclusively by women, and in the Kennebunks, local women often ran them out of their homes. A selection of loose or bagged teas accompanied a tray of sweets or slices of cake and pie. There was a healthy competition among the ladies, each wanting to be considered the finest baker (or to have been savvy enough to have employed the finest baker!).

In direct opposition to what we in America have come to believe, high tea is not actually the aristocratic tea. High tea, sometimes called "meat tea," referred to the main meal of the day for working-class British. Since it was essentially dinner, it was served midday and included meat, potatoes, vegetables, a sweet, and tea. "Low tea" was served late in the afternoon and had been the "invention" of Anna, the Duchess of Bedford (1788–1861). The English had only two meals a day, breakfast and a late dinner, and the poor duchess found herself experiencing a bit of a letdown in the late afternoon. So, she brought European tea service to her rooms at Belvoir Castle, where she invited friends to join her for conversation and sustenance. Since it was the low part of the afternoon, it was named low tea. Hence the tea most of us have always believed to be high tea isn't.

Pearle often talked about the tearooms she visited in the Kennebunks and the foods she ate there, and it was clear to us that it was an important part of her vacation. Sometimes she brought along one or both of her sisters-in-law and my mother remembers joining her once or twice, but most of the time, solitary person that Pearle was, she was just as happy to go off by herself. When my grandmother talked about going for tea, I assumed that there were just the two or three places in the area. I later realized that the Whistling Oyster in Ogunquit and the Bonnie Brig in Kennebunkport, of which she often spoke, were just her favorites. Tearooms had become so popular on the southern coast of Maine that at the zenith of their popularity there were more than a dozen between the Kennebunks, Ogunquit, Wells, and York.

The Rose Grey Tea Room on Summer Street in Kennebunk served a light luncheon featuring lobster salad, as well as an afternoon tea with cakes and light sandwiches of summer cucumber and sweet butter. Many of the rooms held "tea concerts" with a harpist or string quartets, or they planned other diversions for the ladies like bridge tournaments or fashion shows. The Rose Grey, for example, encouraged ladies to entertain their friends with games of mah-jongg, a Jazz Age favorite. Afternoon tea at the Snapdragon Tea Room in Kennebunk meant a "chicken waffle dinner," if one liked. This enormous plate of food consisted of a stack of buttered waffles just off the waffle iron and pieces of freshly butchered chicken from the Snapdragon's farm that were floured, seasoned, and fried until crisp. A pitcher of Maine maple syrup would be put on the table. Everyone ate big, hearty meals in those days, but the men, who would otherwise never set foot in tearooms without being coerced, suddenly got the urge to come for tea when it came with a plate of waffles and fried chicken. Other soul food restaurants around the country are credited with inventing this odd duo in the late 1960s. Yet the dish was advertised in a little Maine newspaper more than forty years before they even opened.

The Whistling Oyster

One of my grandmother's two favorite tearooms was a fifteen-minute car or trolley trip away from Kennebunkport, in the seaside community of Ogunquit. The Whistling Oyster was in a beautiful little shingle house on the village's main road, which led down to the docks and into Perkins Cove, a little artists' colony at the end of the point. By 1924 the Whistling Oyster had already been in business for eighteen years and was still being run by the original owners. The two women ran the tearoom until the early 1940s, by which time, my mom remembers, they were quite elderly. Now the part of the tiny village where the Whistling Oyster stood is packed with gift shops and Barnacle Billy's, a great place for lobsters, steamers, corn on the cob, barbecue chicken and, believe it or not, a terrific piña colada.

Pearle usually made a day of her trip to Ogunquit, which was, and still is, a quaint little town with an impressive art community that has thrived since the 1890s. After tea and sandwiches or a thick wedge of one of their famous berry pies with its slender crust and perfectly sweetened and thickened berries, my grandmother would work off the calories with a walk along the Marginal Way. The thin path of dirt and rocks is a little more than one mile long. It makes its way along dark cliffs that hang above the water with a beach of stones and pebbles below. An Ogunquit farmer, who was worried about the overcommercialization of the beach, left it to the town under the condition that it remain virtually untouched. When I walk that path today, it is as wild and beautiful as it must have been then. Often, I see my grandmother in my mind's eye, walking ahead of me, swift and sure, a solitary figure squinting against the sun and holding her skirt as it blows in the wind, stopping to look at the occasional artist's canvas.

Artists still line up along the water's edge to paint or sell their work in Perkins Cove. After watching the artists Pearle would visit galleries like the Ogunquit Art Association, which was formed in Charles H. Woodbury's studio in 1928. Artists Walt Kuhn, Rockwell Kent, and Marsden Hartley were featured there, as well as lesser-known Ogunquit artists. By the 1950s, Pearle could spend time at the Ogunquit Museum of American Art, considered one of the finest small museums in the country, with works by artists who painted in Maine like Edward Hopper and Andrew Wyeth. Wyeth, now eighty-five, has a long history in Maine, beginning with his illustrator father N. C. Wyeth, who spent much of his life in the tiny fishing village of Port Clyde. In a studio in a farmhouse on a peninsula in midcoast Maine, near the tidal St. George River, Andrew Wyeth painted one of the twentieth century's most famous paintings, *Christina's World,* as well as three hundred more temperas and water colors. Andrew Wyeth's son, painter Jamie Wyeth, is also a Mainer and lives on Monhegan Island, which boasts one of Maine's best-known art colonies.

The Bonnie Brig

Pearle's favorite spot for tea, though, was the Bonnie Brig, run by Mrs. Nan Clark out of her perfect white cottage on Ocean Avenue in Kennebunkport. A beautiful home with dark green shutters, a wide porch that wrapped around the front with green-and-white-striped roll-up awnings, and built-in flower boxes, it was an ideal place for a tearoom. According to town elder and local historian Wallace Reid, Mrs. Clark's husband had been a fisherman who at one point could no longer support them. Fishing was a hard, mean life, with terrible hours and work that didn't stop just because winter forced temperatures to drop well below freezing and nor' easters pummeled the coast.

Sometimes the only thing that kept a man warm out on the rough, icy sea was a drink. So, the Bonnie Brig was not a hobby for Mrs. Clark; it ended up providing sole support for her and her husband for many years.

Besides the evident charm of the Bonnie Brig, it was the fact that Nan Clark was a native of Glasgow that made Pearle feel so comfortable. Pearle and Mrs. Clark spent many hours reminiscing about Glasgow and the breathtaking Scottish countryside. Being Scottish also gave Mrs. Clark a firsthand reference for what the original tearooms were like, so the Bonnie Brig was quite different from other tearooms in the Kennebunkport area.

In the late nineteenth and early twentieth centuries, Glasgow was actually at the center of a revisionist movement in painting, design, and architecture. The legendary Miss Kate Cranston, an avant-garde collector with money and impeccable style, raised the level of tearooms to a new height, bringing in the now legendary designer and architect Charles Rennie Mackintosh to design the rooms for her. Cranston's tearooms became famous throughout Europe, and more than likely, Mrs. Clark visited them. Looking at interior pictures of the Bonnie Brig today, which are unfortunately not clear enough to reproduce, reveals rooms so fresh they seem current. Reviews of the tearoom from the 1920s make special mention of how much more "up-to-date" the room was than its contemporaries, citing its convivial and modern atmosphere and attitude. Baskets sat in the corners and pots of flowers hung in the foyer and over the front fireplaces. The rooms were spare with light-colored walls and molding, and they were filled with a mixture of antique and deco (modern for the time) furniture.

What Mrs. Clark really became famous for, however, was not decoration but food. There were scones from an old family recipe that were pale ivory, soft, and studded with currants or wild Maine blueberries when they were in season. Clotted cream was not available in the States the way it was in Scotland, so she made her own. In her gift shop she sold homemade fudge and salted nuts, delicate sandwiches and tea cakes, and an array of unusual souvenirs. If there was a birthday, you could order one of her famous cakes, and if you were off for a river excursion, she would pack a picnic for you with a smattering of all she had to offer. Even today natives who were just children when the Bonnie Brig was open recall the amazing feats of kitchen magic that Mrs. Clark and her cook turned out each day. So famous was her shortbread that seventy years later people still remember what it tasted like. This shortbread isn't the like of anything we are used to; these weren't thin, little tea cookies, but thick squares of real dense and buttery Scottish shortbread, moist, crumbly, and cakey.

At a time when women coveted their recipes, when half a teaspoon of cinnamon could be the difference between a blue-ribbon apple pie at the local fair and runner-up, Nan did a generous thing: She shared her shortbread recipe with Pearle and her other guests. Pearle made this shortbread for nearly sixty years and each holiday season, and at other times throughout the year, she would present her friends and members of the City Opera company with boxes of the shortbread. One of her biggest fans was opera legend Beverly Sills, who, although she received it more frequently than others did, always eagerly awaited her next gift of shortbread. When my grandmother visited our home in New Rochelle, she would bring us boxes of shortbread and other kinds of cookies, layered carefully between small sheets of wax paper.

A few years ago I wanted to make the shortbread for a dinner at the Beard House and my mom found the original recipe, written out in Pearle's

Pearle and Beverly Sills getting ready to perform at City Opera, circa 1970.

handwriting. I have tried for years to make the shortbread as perfect as my grandmother but to no avail—for something with so few ingredients, you can't believe how hard it is to make well. Pearle became as famous as Mrs. Clark for the shortbread, but she never forgot to give credit to her friend in Kennebunkport.

DESSERTS

Pearle's Shortbread
Makes 1 dozen

Making good shortbread is harder than it seems, but through painful trial and error, I discovered tips that work well, which I've incorporated into the recipe.

1/2 pound (2 sticks) unsalted butter, at room temperature
1/2 cup sugar
2 1/2 cups unbleached all-purpose flour
1/4 teaspoon salt

Preheat the oven to 250°F. Make sure the butter is soft (the higher quality the butter, the better the shortbread). Using a mixer, in a large bowl, cream the butter and sugar until light and fluffy. Gradually add the flour by hand, being very careful not to overmix it since the batter toughens easily. When the flour is incorporated, spread the dough evenly in a 7-inch square pan (the best size for this recipe, but an 8-inch square pan will do). Score the dough lightly with a knife into 2-inch squares. Using a fork, prick two sets of holes evenly into each square. Bake for 45 to 50 minutes, rotating it halfway through, until very pale gold on the edges. It should not brown. Check it occasionally, because all ovens heat differently and it is important not to overbake the shortbread. As soon as you take it from the oven, cut the shortbread along the scoring lines you made earlier. If you wait until it cools, you will have trouble cutting the shortbread without turning it into a crumbly mess.

The Wild Maine Blueberry

Fall foliage in Maine is a miracle. The maple leaves turn from green to orange to deep maroon; the rail-like white birch trees have a shock of yellow at their tops; the slender grasses of the ponds and salt marshes are the color of ripe cantaloupe. But first-time leaf peepers—that's what we call the folks who come up to see the fall foliage—often get a view they never expected. In late autumn Maine's wild blueberry bushes turn the fields a shocking shade of scarlet.

The wild Maine blueberry is a diminutive jewel, grown on low bushes, not like the larger high bush blueberries we get in the grocery stores year-round. They also grow in the wild and prefer wet, boggy habitats. When cooked into jams, chutneys, or jellies or baked in breads, cakes, and pies, they are sweeter, more tender, and hold their color and shape better than the larger berries.

Blueberry Crumble Pie

Serves 8 to 10

This recipe is best served warm with a scoop of vanilla ice cream.

For the crust

2 cups all-purpose flour
$1/2$ teaspoon salt
2 sticks cold butter, cut into tiny pieces
$1/4$ cup ice water

For the crumble

$1^1/2$ cups flour
1 cup firmly packed dark brown sugar
$1^1/2$ sticks sweet butter, cut into little pieces

For the filling

3 pints blueberries, wild Maine if you can get them

1 cup granulated sugar

4 teaspoons cornstarch

$^1/_2$ teaspoon finely chopped lemon zest

Pinch of freshly ground black pepper

To make the crust, combine the flour, salt, and cold butter in a food processor by pulsing until the mixture has the consistency of sand. Add the cold water while pulsing until the mixture comes together; don't overwork it. (To mix the dough by hand, combine the flour, salt, and butter in a large bowl. Add the cold water and work by hand until the mixture comes together.) Remove the dough from the food processor or bowl and on a lightly floured counter or board, shape it into a disk about $^1/_2$ inch thick. Wrap with plastic film and refrigerate for at least 1 hour before rolling it out.

To make the crumble, mix the flour and brown sugar in a food processor until thoroughly combined. Add the butter and pulse until the mixture forms a crumble (do not overwork the mixture). Refrigerate until you are ready to use it.

To make the fruit filling, in a large bowl, mix all the ingredients well. I crush about 20 percent of the blueberries so the juice mixes with the cornstarch and thickens the filling.

To make the pie, preheat the oven to 350°F. Roll out the dough on a floured surface, place in a pie plate, trim, and crimp the edges. Use a fork to poke holes around the sides and bottom of the crust. Cover with a piece of parchment paper and fill it with dried beans. Bake for 8 minutes, or until the crimped edges are firm. Remove the paper and beans and bake for 3 to 5 more minutes to firm the bottom. Fill the crust with the berry mixture, spread out the mixture, and top the pie generously with the crumble. Bake for 1 hour, or until the filling starts to bubble. Cool on a rack.

Blueberry Bread Pudding with Vanilla Custard Sauce

Serves 8

3 tablespoons unsalted butter

6 Pepperidge Farm hot dog buns, top split, if possible

16 egg yolks

1 cup sugar

Pinch of kosher salt

1 vanilla bean, pod split in half lengthwise

1 cup milk

1 quart heavy cream

2 pints blueberries

1 teaspoon finely chopped lemon zest

Preheat the oven to 350°F.

In an ovenproof skillet—in batches if necessary—melt the butter over medium heat and toast the buns on both outer sides until they are golden brown. To dry them out a little, open the buns so that the interiors are exposed and put the skillet in the oven for about 10 minutes.

In a large bowl, whisk together the eggs, sugar, and salt. Scrape the seeds from the vanilla bean with the back of a knife and place the beans and the pod into a large saucepan. Mix in the milk and cream. Scald the mixture over high heat until bubbles start to form around the sides, about 5 minutes. Add a cup of the cream mixture to the egg mixture, whisking constantly to temper it. Whisk the egg mixture into the remaining cream mixture.

Divide the cream mixture into two bowls. Refrigerate the half that doesn't have the vanilla bean in it until you are ready to assemble the pudding. Place the bowl with the vanilla bean in it on top of a pot of simmering water to form a double boiler. With a towel in one hand and a rubber spatula in the other, hold the bowl while continually stirring the mixture, scraping down the sides as you go. It will start to steam and after about 10 minutes will get thick enough to coat the spatula. You should be able to make a finger trail that doesn't lose its shape down the middle of the spatula. Strain the mixture and refrigerate until cool.

Butter a cake or loaf pan, whatever you have that is large enough to hold all the ingredients. Tear the hot dog buns into small pieces and place them in the pan. Add the blueberries. Sprinkle with the lemon zest. Pour two thirds of the thickened cream mixture evenly into the pan, pressing it down with a spatula so that the cream is equally absorbed. Let it stand for 30 minutes, until the cream is completely absorbed. Poke some finger holes every few inches and pour the rest of the thickened cream mixture over it. Cover with aluminum foil and place the loaf pan into a larger roasting pan. Pour water in the pan so that it reaches halfway up the side of the smaller pan. Bake for about 45 minutes. Uncover and bake for another 15 minutes, or until the pudding has set. Serve at room temperature or slightly warm. Dig the pudding out of the pan with a large spoon and serve it in soup bowls, with the reserved cream mixture ladled over and around it.

Blackberry Nectarine Crisp

Serves 6

For the crisp

$1/4$ cup all-purpose flour

$1/2$ cup oats

$1/2$ cup firmly packed light brown sugar

$1/4$ teaspoon ground cinnamon

$1/4$ teaspoon salt

6 tablespoons ($3/4$ stick) unsalted butter

2 cups whole blackberries

3 cups nectarines, pitted, peeled, and cut into 1-inch chunks

$1/2$ cup granulated sugar

$1/2$ teaspoon vanilla extract

Butter a 2-quart baking dish. Preheat the oven to 375°F.

To make the crisp, in a food processor, mix the flour, oats, sugar, cinnamon, and salt. Add the butter and pulse until the mixture comes together.

To make the filling, in a large bowl, combine the blackberries, nectarines, granulated sugar, and vanilla. Pour the filling into the baking dish and cover with the crisp mixture. Bake for 50 minutes, or until it starts bubbling.

Variation: For a Strawberry Rhubarb Crisp, substitute 3 cups rhubarb, cut into 1-inch chunks, and 2 cups strawberries, halved and quartered, for the nectarines and blackberries.

Maine Maple Crème Brûlée

Serves 4

8 egg yolks

$1/2$ cup sugar (plus 4 tablespoons for topping)

2 tablespoons maple syrup

2 vanilla beans, pods split lengthwise

$2 1/2$ cups heavy cream

Preheat the oven to 350°F.

In a large bowl, mix the egg yolks, $1/2$ cup sugar, and the maple syrup. Scrape the vanilla beans and place the beans and the pod into a small saucepan. Add the cream and scald the cream and vanilla beans over high heat. Slowly add a cup of the cream mixture to the egg mixture, whisking constantly to temper it. Whisk the egg mixture into the remaining cream mixture. Remove the vanilla beans with a slotted spoon and pour the mixture into four 4-ounce ramekins or small bowls. Place the ramekins in a roasting pan and put the pan in the oven. Pour water into the roasting pan until it's halfway up the sides of the ramekins. Bake for 1 hour, or until the custard has set.

Refrigerate until ready to serve. Before serving, sprinkle the top of the custard with the remaining sugar. Use a small kitchen blowtorch to caramelize the sugar into a hard crust.

New England Rolls: Lobster Roll,
Fried Clam Roll, and Shrimp Salad Roll
with Coleslaw and Overnight Pickles

**Pearl Oyster Bar Lobster Roll
with Shoestring Fries**

Lobster Chef Salad

The Classic Shore Dinner: Clam Chowder, Steamers, Lobster, Grilled Corn with an Heirloom Tomato Salad

**Malpeque Oysters on the Half Shell
with Mignonette and Pearl Oyster Bar
Cocktail Sauce**

**Taylor Bay Scallops
in the Shell with Leeks
and Butter Sauce**

Pearle's Shortbread

Blueberry Crumble Pie

Twilight Time

WHEN YOU'RE AT THE BEACH, THERE IS SOMETHING ABOUT THE WINDING DOWN OF THE DAY THAT IS PARTICULARLY SPECIAL. As much of a morning person as Pearle was, I know she felt it, too. From six o'clock in the evening, when the sun hangs low and the white shadow of a pale moon can be seen on the horizon, the evening grows increasingly lovely.

After cleaning up, we make a shaker of cocktails and rush over to Middle Beach, the best place to see most of the sunset, torturously around the corner and just out of full view. Some nights you actually get to see the sun slipping down, a hot magenta ball melting into the water, letting all fishermen know that the next

day will be a fine one for sailing. On other nights, the sunset is just a hazy glow that lights the entire back of the ocean and then sort of slips away, leaving behind the dazzling part of the day, twilight.

Pearle and Ellie take a break during a walk on Gooch's Beach, August 1928.

The Front Porch

Supper was served early at the Forest Hill House. By six o'clock, Rosa had the pickles and salads, vegetables and homemade breads set out on the table and the fish or meats on the sideboard ready to be served when the guests came in. My mother says they were enormous meals during which there was lively conversation with the other families or among themselves.

After dinner, the conversation was carried out to one of the two major social hubs, the parlor or porch. Today, the two porches remain, a sweeping one that wraps almost entirely around the annex and a small one on what was the main farmhouse. Forest Hill's parlor had a Victrola with both records for the latest dance crazes such as the Charleston and more classical fare. If you did stay to yourself in your room, which was probably too hot anyway, you were looked at askance.

When Pearle visited Forest Hill for the first time, the prosperity of the 1920s had afforded the Toothakers the opportunity to provide the guests with more to do, and in the evenings, Forest Hill actually offered quite a few entertainment options. Dinner was over by seven and with a few more hours of light, the men would sometimes play horseshoes on the lawn, families might play croquet, or couples would put on their tennis whites and use the red clay tennis court. There was also the dance hall, a large building in the back where performances of traveling vaudeville acts and dances were held. On warm summer nights, kids staying at Forest Hill would lie in bed and listen to music for the foxtrot and the Charleston, which had become famous in the 1923 *Ziegfeld Follies* on Broadway. On other nights it was set up for tournaments of bridge or gin and mah-jongg.

Fireflies and Peppermint Ice Cream

After dinner my family usually continued their conversations on one of the porches before going in to sit in the parlor until bedtime. My grandparents rocked back and forth in the enormous wicker rocking chairs eating dessert, while my mother and her cousins sat on the edge of the porch, swinging their legs, and devoured towering layers of cake or slabs of pie with ice cream melting down the sides. Then they'd dart around the lawn, making the most of those last precious moments before they had to go to bed, running through the honeysuckle bushes catching fireflies in jelly jars that Rosa gave them with holes punched in the tops, or playing hide-and-seek in the dark.

My family didn't always eat at the hotel. Some nights they would dress for dinner and head down to the beach toward the sunset. The kids would play tag while the adults strolled and discussed where they would go that evening for dinner. By then there were quite a few popular places to eat; clam shacks offered buckets of steamers, fried fish sandwiches, platters of fried oysters or clams, and cups of chowders.

There were down-home establishments that served plain, home-cooked food that reminded visitors of their own kitchens and restaurants that specialized in fine dining. Mrs. Barbara Collier, a docent for Kennebunk's Brickstore Museum, waited tables as a teenager in the early 1930s, at the Griste Mill, a decades-old working gristmill that had been turned into a restaurant. She says that when the Goldsmiths ate there, they would have had a wide choice that included halibut, swordfish, lobster thermidor, or steak. But the most popular meal by far was the classic shore dinner. For $2.50 diners began with a fruit cup and then had their choice of lobster stew or clam chowder. Next came steamed clams, and finally a boiled lobster served with French fries or mashed potatoes, peas, or carrots in ginger sauce. In mid-August, the vegetable selection would feature corn, on the cob or in a succotash. Dessert was a choice among pies, cakes, puddings, homemade ice cream, and fruit. My mother doesn't remember her first lobster; she was so young when she ate it. But she remembers grappling with their hard, uncooperative shells while she was still so little her feet didn't reach the floor when she sat in a chair.

A decade earlier when my grandparents and aunt and uncle went out, they could stay in Kennebunkport and go to the Parker House for different kinds of fresh fish, fish cakes, and baked beans. Over in Cape Porpoise, a ten-minute drive down the road, they could go to the restaurant at the Lansford House hotel, which also had a particularly good shore dinner but, like most other restaurants at that time, also offered a good sirloin steak or the very popular Vermont roast turkey.

On other nights Pearle, who loved to walk, would spearhead a family walk down to Dock Square after dinner to walk around the town. In the evenings there were often band concerts and the music would follow them around the square as they stopped to gaze at store windows, or eat one of many confections they would have found at the well-loved Young's Ice Cream Shop. Back then, culture was not geared toward kids the way it is now: There were no toy mega-stores or stacks of candies at every store. They did not get allowances, at least the Goldsmith children didn't. On vacation they might get a nickel each week to spend in town, but even that, as my mother recalls, was a momentous event.

Young's had an old-time soda fountain and an array of penny candies and confections lining the walls. Malteds and ice cream floats, as well as sundaes with hot fudge, strawberry, butterscotch, or marshmallow toppings, and milkshakes were available at the counter. Homemade fudge and saltwater taffy, both famous seashore treats, rounded out the choice. It was a veritable *Willy Wonka and the Chocolate Factory,* and the children would sometimes spend over an hour choosing while the adults strolled around the village.

Grown-Ups

Some nights Goldie and Pearle and Sam and Jenny needed time without the children. On these nights, Sam and Goldie's sister, Flora, or the oldest cousin, Gertrude, would stay back at the Forest Hill House and baby-sit. I enjoy the idea of my grandparents and aunt and uncle sneaking into some juke joint several miles out of the Kennebunks to have a few cocktails and listen to some music. It's a pretty romantic notion but one that keeps them young in a part of my mind. Otherwise, my memories of Pearle would always be of a formidable little old lady, and my grandfather, sadly, a virtual ghost, having died from leukemia when I was only three.

When they dined in more expensive restaurants, it was much like it is today: the safest bet is to order the lobster. The Old Fort Inn in Kennebunkport had an eclectic menu that included lots of Maine seafood as well as baked rice cakes with raisins and boiled lambs' tongues vinaigrette. The Playhouse Inn held regular dances and then served suppers à la carte, prepared by their new chef who, in 1924, had just come from the Waldorf-Astoria in New York.

Casinos were incredibly popular at the time, not casinos in the way we think of them today, but popular places to go listen to orchestras, have something to eat, and dance the night away. By all accounts, Pearle and Goldie cut a fine rug, and the two couples liked to spend at least a few warm summer nights on the dance floor. The Beachwood Casino's 1924 season offered dancing to jazz bands and orchestras every Saturday and Wednesday night. Island Ledge Casino in Wells Beach featured Frankie Ward and his orchestra on Tuesday, Thursday, and Saturday nights, though it was a little less exclusive and catered to a much larger crowd. The Cape Porpoise Casino was not an elegant affair either, but it was different from Island Ledge, fun and on the water. They served an extensive seafood menu and a much loved shore dinner that included steamed clams *and* fried clams, clam chowder or lobster stew, and lobster salad, or a broiled lobster for an extra sixty cents.

The Twilight of Goldie and Pearle

My grandmother had begun singing opera professionally in 1930 and a decade later she was crossing the country every year with the touring company. Unfortunately this meant that her opportunity to vacation was cut down considerably. Goldie and Pearle still summered in Maine, still stayed at Forest Hill, but usually not for an entire month. When Sam and Goldie could still coordinate their schedules, which they tried hard to do, the kids had their own lives. By the time she was eleven or twelve, my mother started going to camp in Maine instead of staying with her parents at the Forest Hill House. The Highland Nature Camp was situated on Lake Sebago and drew other New York City girls like fellow camper Betty Perske, who grew up to be Lauren Bacall.

During World War II, Sam wasn't even around, having become an officer and spending much of the early 1940s in various European countries. Things in Maine had changed too, and like most people we are not a family much interested in change, particularly when it means the loss of things we have enjoyed. The bathhouses went, as did the tearooms, which must have made my grandmother particularly sad.

The 1950s should have brought more golden, happy times to Pearle and Goldie. They weathered the financial and emotional storms of their early years of marriage. Goldie was a greatly loved and enormously successful figure in New York City Jewish social organizations and fund-raising circles, while Pearle had her career with the Metropolitan Opera. My brother David and I saw them often, and when I was going through the family trunks looking for our history, I found a wonderful old sterling key chain engraved with the phrase HIYA' BRAMPA. Although I remember very little about him, seeing that key chain brought back this vague, warm remembrance, and I realized what a special person he must have been to us.

I would never get the chance to know him as I would have liked. Around 1956, he had begun a battle with leukemia that he eventually lost. There was very little they could do back then for the disease, most of it amounting to blood transfusions. Goldie fought the disease for a couple of years, and I can just barely make out the memory of sitting at his bedside when he was particularly ill. Pearle and Goldie tried hard to keep to their social routine despite his health, and in the summer of 1958 they decided to go up to Maine.

It had been thirty-eight years since that first summer they visited Kennebunkport. Letters Pearle wrote from this time say that she hoped a trip to the seashore would be restorative for Goldie, and they had planned to stay for several weeks, relaxing and enjoying the sea breezes. But just a few days after they arrived, my grandfather became gravely ill and was taken to a Portland hospital. He died there within days. My grandmother brought him back by train and buried him in Brooklyn.

Pearle's life, of course, was never the same again. She had always been a solitary person but my grandfather, who was bigger than life, could draw her out and make her laugh in spite of herself. Although she didn't shoo us away, she didn't go searching for company either, and it seems that her isolation increased enormously. By the time my grandmother passed away, she had been without my grandfather for over thirty years. I think she missed him terribly, and when I was going through some family pictures I found some of the touching and humbling letters of condolence my grandmother received after his death.

Although her stoicism probably wouldn't ever allow her to admit it, she was clearly undone by his loss, by the loss of what was truly her other half. In contrast to my wonderful, but rather serious grandmother, my grandfather laughed easily, had a fast wit and a ready smile. He befriended everyone, and they lit up when he walked into the room. Opposites either work well or turn into a nightmare. For Goldie and Pearle it seemed to work well.

Pearle continued to visit Maine every year. Sometimes she would go by herself, a solitary figure walking on the beach, rocking on the porch, or having her dinner at a local restaurant after Forest Hill had stopped serving meals. At other times she would go up when Sam and Jenny planned to be there. They managed to get there nearly every year during the 1950s and 1960s, usually with their daughter Gertrude and her daughters Louise and Erika. Louise remembers, "We didn't so much go with Aunt Bec as we kind of . . . met up with her. She was so cool, always going off on her own to do her errands, take her walks, or visit with the people she had come to know in town. Then we would wander down to the beach or be at the door to go to dinner, and she would mysteriously appear."

Louise vividly recalls Pearle teaching her to crochet in the parlor on damp summer nights when it was too sticky or too buggy to be outside. "Aunt Bec was my very favorite person of all the family. Everybody else could be a little . . . larger than life, a little self-congratulatory," she says, laughing. "But Aunt Bec was elegant and a straight shooter. She always spoke to kids as if they were small adults who deserved respect. We'd sit there in the Forest Hill parlor every night and she would teach me to crochet. I loved those evenings because everyone was together."

But my parents and brother and I weren't there quite as often, certainly not as often as the Goldsmith-Charles women would have liked. By the beginning of the 1950s my mother had married my father and by 1954, they had had David and myself. We were a suburban family at the height of the Eisenhower and television years, and life was lived much differently than it had been when my grandparents were a young couple. My dad worked long hours at NBC and got only minimal vacation time. We were kids with ball games and music lessons and camp to attend. We wanted to spend time with our friends instead of our family, not knowing (how could we?) that one day it would be those times with our family that we would treasure more than anything.

Over the years my mom and I have become quite close. We see each other often, go to the theater, and make dinners at her home in Connecticut. My brother and his family live in Maison Lafitte outside of Paris, and I have often wished they didn't live so far away because we don't get to see them as often as I would like. For several years we celebrated Christmas in Maine, at the house my mom bought, and when we did, we would make my grandmother's goose or my favorite holiday meal, standing rib roast, glistening with its own juices. One year our Christmas tree came from our lawn, the kind of thing that can happen only in a place like Maine. There was an enormous blue spruce that my mom thought was too close to the house, and since we had extraordinarily high ceilings, I cut it down with the chain saw, brought it inside, and we had the most beautiful tree ever. It is true that you miss everyone more as you get older and realize that you have missed out on so much. I wish my grandparents were here now and that we could all go up once more for a summer vacation to Kennebunkport.

Hot Fudge Sauce

Serves 4

Over the last twenty years I have had no fewer than five different alleged recipes for Schrafft's hot fudge sauce. After days, months, and years of testing and tasting, I can tell you that none of them were it. It's grown into a huge frustration for me, because I grew up on Schrafft's hot fudge. Then the flavor had such depth and texture, which started out hot and gooey but turned chewy as soon as it hit the ice cream.

There were two Schrafft's restaurants that I got to know well. One was in midtown Manhattan, but the one I frequented was in downtown New Rochelle, where I would sit at the counter with my best friend, Margie Hornick, before the movies, eating a hot fudge sundae while she had the black and white soda.

When I first started serving hot fudge at Pearl, we had just opened and I could not get the recipe right. Not that I'm *that* much of a purist, but it is hard for me to serve something when I know it isn't right. So I took it off the menu. I recently came up with an amalgam of all of the recipes I've had plus my memory, and I'm pretty happy with it. But it still drives me a little crazy, because I know that somewhere out there someone knows the real recipe!

2 cups heavy cream

$^1/_2$ cup firmly packed brown sugar

2 tablespoons cocoa powder

4 ounces unsweetened chocolate

4 or 5 shakes of malt vinegar

$^1/_2$ teaspoon salt

3 tablespoons light corn syrup

4 tablespoons ($^1/_2$ stick) unsalted butter

2 teaspoons good-quality vanilla extract

In a medium saucepan over low heat, whisk together the heavy cream and brown sugar until the sugar dissolves, about 4 to 5 minutes. Add the cocoa powder and whisk to combine. Add the chocolate and whisk until it's melted. Add the vinegar, salt, corn syrup, and butter, a small piece at a time, whisking constantly. Simmer the mixture for 10 minutes, stirring often. If the mixture seems too thick, add a little heavy cream. Stir in the vanilla extract. Pour the mixture into a container and keep it warm in a water bath for immediate use or refrigerate. It will keep for up to a week.

Butterscotch Praline Parfait
Serves 4 to 6

Cooking should be a fun experience that's about more than simply following a recipe. That's why I like to teach the basics and then encourage people to feel their way around and create their own recipes. Making brittle is an example of this. It's a versatile sweet that you can put your own mark on once you understand the basics of making it. You can cook the sugar longer to make a darker brittle, which I like, or you can make a lighter colored brittle with a gentler flavor. You can use a variety of nuts. By changing the pan size, you can make it as thick or thin as you like.

If you're going to serve it on ice cream sundaes, the best thing to do is chop it into bite-sized pieces. But you can also crunch it up pebble size and bake it into cookies in addition to or instead of chocolate chips. Brittle also makes a terrific gift and will last if it is kept in a tightly closed container in a dry place. The only problem with brittle is that it takes longer to dry on humid days.

I'm not prone to buying lots of kitchen gadgets. Perhaps it's because I live in New York City, where space is at a premium and you don't have lots of extra drawers and surfaces in your kitchen. But if you're going to be making brittle frequently, a candy thermometer is a solid, inexpensive investment.

Caution: Working with hot sugar can be very dangerous. Be very careful not to spill it or get any on your skin.

For the butterscotch

1/2 pound firmly packed light brown sugar

4 teaspoons butter, softened

1¾ cups heavy cream

For the brittle

2 pounds chopped pecans

1 pound sugar

To make the butterscotch, in a large saucepan over high heat, combine the brown sugar and 1/4 cup water and boil the mixture until it's thick and foamy. Remove the mixture from the heat and add the butter, swirling the pan until the butter is entirely melted. Return it to the burner, add the heavy cream, and bring the mixture to a boil. Reduce the mixture until it is slightly thickened, about 2 to 3 minutes. Store in a warm water bath for immediate use or in a container in the refrigerator. It will keep for about a week. Reheat it in a double boiler or hot water bath and serve warm over ice cream with the praline.

To make the brittle, preheat the oven to 350°F. Toast the pecans in a 14 x 10-inch roasting pan for 5 minutes, shaking the nuts once or twice so they don't burn. Put them aside. In a large saucepan over high heat, bring the sugar and 1/2 cup water to a boil and continue to boil for 8 to 10 minutes. The sugar will go through varying stages of brown from lighter to darker. Once it starts to brown, don't take your eyes off the mixture because it burns easily. The mixture will foam up after about 10 minutes and should be mahogany in color—walnut means you have gone too far. If you're using a candy thermometer, it should reach 340°F. Stir with a wooden spoon or carefully swirl the pan a couple of times during this process to ensure even coloration. Immediately, slowly and very carefully, pour the mixture over the pecans, coating all the nuts. Let the brittle cool completely, about 2 hours. Invert the pan and whack the bottom with something heavy (I use the butt of a chef's knife) to get the brittle out of the pan and then break the praline into chunks. (It stores better in large chunks, but for the parfait you will need smaller chunks.) Leftover brittle can be stored in an airtight container at room temperature.

Maine Blueberry Sauce

Makes about 1 cup

This is a very fresh fruit sauce meant for ice cream, so you don't have to cook it too much. The method can be applied to raspberries and blackberries as well.

1 pint blueberries
1 tablespoon sugar
A squeeze of fresh lemon juice or a little finely chopped lemon zest

Put the blackberries in a medium saucepan over low heat and crush one quarter of them with the back of a spoon. Add the sugar (more than 1 tablespoon if the blueberries are tart) and simmer the mixture for 3 to 4 minutes, or until the blueberries are soft enough to push through a strainer. Stir in the lemon juice. Force the mixture through a fine strainer. Refrigerate until ready to use.

PART THREE

My Mother
and Me

The 1950s

THERE ARE COUPLES WHO DEFINE THE IDEA THAT OPPOSITES ATTRACT, AND MY GRANDPARENTS WERE JUST SUCH A COUPLE.

Pearle was reserved, Goldie effusive, but it was a good match and they had fun together. My mother and father were opposites too, drawn to each by some strange magnetic pull of positive and negative. A decade into their marriage, however, the fun began to ebb.

When my mother was young she had trained as, and wanted to be, a dancer. Pearle, however, did not approve. She wanted my mother to be a concert pianist. Instead of either, my mother went to Syracuse University and concentrated on her talents as an artist, and a considerable talent it was too. By the time she was in her early twenties, she was working for Brooks Costume Company, a famous Broadway costumer. At only twenty-four years old, she was the designer for the original Broadway show *Finian's Rainbow*. Both the production and my mother's costumes were a smash. One night after the show's debut, Mom walked into Sardi's, a theater district restaurant where many of the opening night parties were held. She was with my grandparents. Sitting at a table was the legendary Cole Porter, and when they were introduced, Mr. Porter complimented the splendid job my mother

A publicity still of my mom from 1947. She had just designed the costumes for *Finian's Rainbow*.

had done on *Finian*. Had she continued, who knows what her career would have been like?

But one night, as rehearsals were about to begin on *Finian's Rainbow,* my mother met a dashing man with impossibly dark eyes and wavy dark hair, and they swept one another off their feet. At the time, my father was the assistant stage manager and pictures of them show a handsome young couple, deeply in love. My parents may have ended up in the same environment, but they came from very different places. And unlike Pearle and Goldie, they were oil and water.

My dad, George Charles, and my mom when they were dating in the late 1940s.

My dad, George Charles, was a first-generation American, whose parents were born in the Arab country of Syria. He grew up in the poverty-stricken coal-mine area of western Pennsylvania. To get what little they had, his family struggled in the mines, breathing lungs full of life-choking, black dust twelve to fifteen hours a day. Family life was difficult. His father was violent, and my dad ran away from home when he was just fifteen and fended for himself for the rest of his life. After serving in World War II, he managed to go to college on the GI bill, which was really the only way he could have paid for it. He put in two years at Ithaca College (not far from my grandfather's alma mater) before going on to Yale University's acclaimed drama school. He must have wanted to be an actor, but he made his living as a stage manager. As far back as I can remember, he always had a cigarette in one hand and a cocktail in the other. His dark hair had flecks of gray early on, and his nervous energy—and the cigarettes—kept him thin, almost gaunt at times.

He looked older, more worn, than my fresh-faced mother, who was just a few years younger.

My mother was a product of New York City's Upper West Side, born into a hardworking family who believed in education. My mom had camp and Kennebunkport in the summer, and dance, music, and art lessons during the year. Her parents were incredibly polished, successful people and so they emphasized success. They were never happy about my mom and dad's relationship, but in 1949 my parents married anyway. My brother David came along in 1952, followed by me in 1954.

The Petries

After their wedding, my parents left the theater. My mother became a housewife, and my dad went to work in the relatively new medium of television. He worked on several shows for NBC, including *Today* and *The Tonight Show* (when it was still filmed in New York).

They settled in New Rochelle, where I grew up, not far from Carl Reiner and his family. Mr. Reiner transformed his experiences as a comedy writer liv-

---

Cheesies

Makes about 1 dozen

$1/2$ cup mayonnaise

2 tablespoons freshly grated Parmesan cheese

1 tablespoon finely minced onion

1 teaspoon finely chopped parsley

Pinch of kosher salt and freshly ground black pepper

1 package cocktail rye bread (or larger rye slices cut in thirds)

In a large bowl, combine the mayonnaise, Parmesan, onion, parsley, and salt and pepper. Spread the mixture generously on the bread slices. Broil or bake (at 450°F) the slices until golden brown and bubbly, about 3 to 4 minutes. Serve with cocktails.

---

ing in the suburbs and commuting to Manhattan each day to *The Dick Van Dyke Show*. In the show he played Alan Brady, but he was actually more like the Rob Petrie character. My parents were friendly with the Reiners, and in a way we all lived that Rob, Laura, and Ritchie Petrie life. Each morning the neighborhood

My family in front of the beach house on Gooch's Beach, 1967. From the left, Uncle Sam, Aunt Jenny, Grandma and, David, Mom, and me in front.

men, including my dad, took the same train into Manhattan to go to work, many of them in different areas of show business. The wives threw cocktail parties and exchanged recipes, including a great recipe for cheesies that Estelle Reiner gave my mom in the early 1960s. Many Christmases, Mr. Reiner would dress up as Santa and all of the kids, me included, would take turns having our picture taken sitting on Santa's lap.

Apthorp Days

If I recall correctly, the Petries were partial to the Catskills, but in the 1950s and 1960s my family continued to go up to Kennebunkport every summer. Early in their marriage, my mom took her new husband there, and we went back again off and on throughout my childhood. My grandmother, I think, was very happy to have us there with her. She had played with my mother on the beach and now, though she wasn't as agile as she was in her twenties, she walked all over it with us. Sometimes my cousins Erika and Louise were there, but for the most part, it was just David and me playing together. We went looking for shipwrecks, built sand castles, and explored underneath the old beach house—just as my mother and her cousins had. It is strange looking at those pictures because my dad seems out of place at the beach. Wearing black loafers, tailored pants, and a V-neck sweater, he looks more like he is about to go onstage with Frank Sinatra, Dean Martin, and Sammy Davis Jr. than walk on Gooch's Beach.

My parents' marriage was nothing like the Petries' ideal partnership, however, and it ended in an ugly divorce in the 1970s. Their marriage took a toll on all of us, and I was estranged at different times from both my mom and dad. (I discovered my father's death in the late 1980s quite by accident. I had gone looking for him at NBC, hoping that we might see each other and put the past behind us. Unfortunately, it was already behind me; I just didn't know it.)

David and me at the Apthorp with Pearl.

Although in my mind my grandmother is forever associated with Kennebunkport, my first real memories of her are not from Maine. When my mother and father needed time alone and just couldn't stand David and me another minute, my mother would load us into the car and drive us into Manhattan to stay the night with Pearle. These were magical nights for me—even though on the way there I always suffered carsickness of epic proportions. By the time the lights on the George Washington Bridge were in view, my mother would have to pull over and let me out.

Our drive continued along the upper part of the West Side Highway, sidled up against the Hudson River, until we reached the Seventy-Ninth Street

Boat Basin exit. The sailboats drifted like balloons, anchored to heavy ropes out in the water. When I drive on that part of the highway today, I feel that childhood excitement all over again. But the pitching navy Hudson River paled in my young mind as soon as my mother drove the station wagon into the Apthorp's huge gated stone courtyard. No matter when we arrived, it was still and hushed, and time just seemed to stop.

An old Renaissance building from the turn of the last century owned by the heirs of the John Jacob Astor estate, the Apthorp covers the block from Seventy-Eighth to Seventy-Ninth streets, from Broadway to West End Avenue. Being inside the Apthorp was like being inside the walls of a small kingdom. For David and me, it was like being in a castle. Ancient elevators with heavy wood carvings were hand-run by uniformed elevator operators who had the precision of today's air traffic controllers; up a little too high, down a smidgen past the floor, settling at last evenly with the floor you wanted. It was a lovely little dance that is all but forgotten now, and had there been no elevator operators, we would have been hard-pressed to get up and down. My brother David and I had a little song about it, Harry Belafonte style: "Push de button, up goes the elevator, push de button, down goes the elevator. . . ." We had great adventures on those elevators, wandering around the courtyard, or dropping water on the heads of unsuspecting passersby from Grandma's bathroom window overlooking Broadway.

If I close my eyes I can see her apartment, right down to the way every piece of furniture was arranged in her living room. She loved contraption fur-niture that had more than one use or could be folded into smaller, easier-to-hide pieces. She had a wonderful "chair table" that was always a source of won-der for my brother and me. When we came to visit it was used as a cocktail table, and then when the shrimp and chopped liver were whisked away, it turned into a very low chair—perfect for a child. She really understood the practical aspects of living in a New York City apartment, even though by today's standards it was pretty large.

Her kitchen was a miracle, or should I say getting around her kitchen was a miracle? To this day I don't know how all of those wonderful meals came from that tiny space. She didn't like people hovering over her as she worked (I inherited this same strain of claustrophobia), so the lack of space was probably a relief for her. She had a squat, white Frigidaire always stocked with real food like farmer cheese and vegetables, and a wall of kitchen cabinets that reached up to the ceiling were always packed with all kinds of foods. There

Pearle in costume at City Opera, circa 1970.

were plenty of staples, like flour and sugar for her baking, but there were also the English, Scottish, and Jewish products of her youth. In keeping with her aforementioned love of contraption furniture, she had an old painted stepladder that was really a marvel of engineering. It folded practically into the size of a loaf of bread and unfolded to reach the uppermost corners of her enormous cabinets.

Every time we visited there were warm cookies waiting for us: thick squares of cakey shortbread, brittle gingersnaps heavy with spice, sugary almond crescents, and David's favorite, peanut butter cookies that were dense, crumbly, and buttery. Before bed, my grandmother would take down the bottle of honey she kept above her Frigidaire, dip in a teaspoon, and put the whole thing in my mouth. I love honey to this day, and the gesture was precious to me because of the understated affection of the moment. At night, she tucked

David and me into the twin beds in her bedroom. She would sit next to one of us, peeling and slicing apples as the light from the hallway fell across our beds. She would pass us these slices until we drifted off to sleep, our mouths sticky and sweet from the snack. As bad as her back was, she always took the couch when we visited.

My grandmother was still working when my brother and I went to stay with her; in fact, after the Met retired her when she was sixty-five, as was their mandatory rule, Pearle went straight to City Center on Fifty-Fifth Street, which housed the New York City Opera, and worked for them. My grandmother had gotten a late start and was not going to stop performing after only thirty-one years. In 1961, when she joined the company's chorus, City Opera may not yet have had the clout the Met enjoyed, but its founders had high hopes that it could combine an innovative and varied repertory while providing affordable opera for a larger audience who normally might not have been able to attend. When Beverly Sills made City Opera her home base in 1966 and the company moved from City Center into the Philip Johnson–designed New York State Theater at Lincoln Center, they were on their way.

Pearle performed with City Opera for over twenty-five years until she finally retired because of heart problems in 1976 at the age of eighty. In her later years, the company treated her like the grande dame she was. When her feet could no longer withstand the several-hour performances, the costume department made special shoes to accommodate her, and sets were fitted with seats that allowed her to get off her feet while she sang. Often nearby chorus members could hear her knitting needles clacking away as she knitted, unseen by the audience.

After my grandmother retired from the City Opera, she was never really the same. She moved to New Rochelle to live with my mom and died within two years. When Mom and I went through Pearle's stuff, we found ourselves looking at memorabilia we had not seen in years: pieces of old costumes, her music scores from performances with notations along the margins, and numerous pictures of her in costume. Vain to the end, she remained protective of her age even in death. In a handwritten note I found on the back of an envelope, she directs my mother to be careful while making funeral arrangements: "Since New York City Opera does not know my legitimate age—do not give my birth date for newspaper purposes or to Rabbi who does the service."

I was in my twenties when my grandmother passed away. Sadly, I was going through a particularly wild period, so we had not seen much of each other in those last years.

Cooking 101

After two years at SUNY Purchase, where my only significant contribution was one really good women's film series—in which I showed everything from Andy Warhol's *Women in Revolt* to the 1937 Katharine Hepburn classic *Stage Door*—I was bored. I thought I wanted to be the American female Ingmar Bergman, that I wanted to direct films. But I had neither the discipline nor the drive necessary to be a filmmaker, especially a woman filmmaker in the pioneer days of the early 1970s. Leaving all of my artistic and motivated friends behind, I barged into the real world and, frankly, we weren't ready for one another.

I was qualified for nothing, as far as a job went, and game for anything, as I had always been when it came to jobs, even in high school. While other girls were baby-sitting, I was packing meat at our local grocery store. They had three or four really good old-time Italian butchers. Al, the head of the department, hired me to pack the meat as they cut it. Greta, the other meat packer, had a heavy accent, but managed to train me nonetheless. Mostly she taught me how to avoid getting hurt while doing it. And there were plenty of ways to get hurt, from burning your fingers on the pricing machine to burning your hands on a hot wire that was used to quick-cut the plastic wrap.

I loved working for those guys. They took great pride in the product they put on the shelves, which was always top quality. The work could be hard, but Al, Tony, and the other guys treated me as an equal even though I was just a high school kid. Every Friday afternoon I was invited to join them in the meat locker, sides of beef and veal and lamb legs hanging around us on giant hooks, for an end-of-the-week drink. Nobody was "partying" or whooping it up, it was just a bunch of middle-aged butchers who had made it through another long week, and me, sitting around drinking shots of Dewars from Dixie cups.

This time when I needed a job after leaving college, my only job offer wasn't nearly as exotic as being a butcher. My best friend, Emily Olshansky, and I had grown up together in New Rochelle, and when I told her that I had left school, she suggested I come and work with her as a bartender in a Manhattan restaurant. Bartending was a cool job, especially for someone in her early twenties. The hours were late and the money was decent if you were any good. The restaurant served a quirky hybrid of Japanese and American food and for the 1970s was considered groundbreaking in many ways. It became so popular that the owner—let's call her Kyoto—opened six or seven around the city. We worked the bar in one of the Greenwich Village locations, which was always busy and open late.

At best, Kyoto's English was serviceable, and since her husband was from South America, it was also speckled with Spanish colloquialisms. She gave us all nicknames, but everybody I knew already called me by a childhood nick-name, Bixie. Kyoto used to scream her version of this, *Da Beecie,* across the kitchen anytime she needed something, and it just made the hair stand straight up on the back of my neck.

Working in the restaurant business, I quickly learned that drinking and staying out late are part of the culture, and I'm sure that's part of what appealed to me. I was also working with Emily, who had been my best friend since high school. We had been thick as thieves then, outlaws on the fringe of suburban high school society. But now finding ourselves in the middle of New York City during the 1970s, we had the opportunity to indulge ourselves in all manner of decadence. Most nights a group of us would leave work well after one o'clock in the morning, go out to the clubs, and get home to our respective beds at dawn. I was enjoying this carefree existence, even if it drove my family completely crazy.

As sexy and fun as it was, bartending would be short-lived for me, though. One day we walked into the restaurant and heard screaming and yelling coming from the kitchen. Not that this was anything new since Kyoto was always fighting with her kitchen staff, but it was of a particularly loud, angry variety and it was in Japanese so we couldn't be sure what was going on. Pretty soon Kyoto came running out, hysterical, and shoved Emily and me into the kitchen. Her entire cooking staff of Chinese men had packed up their cleavers and walked out on her. With less than an hour until opening, Kyoto decided that the three of us were going to cook. Thus began my "career" as a chef.

Kyoto, though one of the most interesting people I have ever met in the food business, could be conniving, vicious, sadistic, and cheap, cheaper than anyone I have ever met. Although she was always concerned about the quality of the food, everything else that wasn't kosher to do in a restaurant, she did. She would buy enormous jugs of the cheapest liquors at discount stores and refill the bottles. At one point the Dewars bottles had been refilled so many times, the labels all peeled off. When Kyoto wanted a good deal at the fish market, she would dress up in her expensive fur coat, make us do our hair and makeup, and take us down to Fulton Street at two in the morning to pimp us for cheaper snapper.

Kyoto's belief was that if we batted our eyes and smiled sweetly, she'd get a better deal from the fishmen. Apparently it worked, because every time she needed fish, I was in the women's room in the middle of the night applying fresh eyeliner and lipstick. Back then the Fulton Street fish market had not been revitalized. There were no shops or quaint lighting, no bus tours or Wall Streeters tipping out of yuppie bars at one o'clock in the morning. Now the Fulton Fish Market is part of the South Street Seaport and wedged between Gap and Sharper Image stores on streets that look like quaint city streets from the nineteenth century. Back then, of course, it was mostly fish guts and teamsters. I will say this, on these trips I learned a lot about buying fresh fish, information I still use today.

After work one night Kyoto told us that she was leaving the Village space and that we needed to help her move. So she sent us home, as if everything was normal, but we were to return in the middle of the night. At 3:00 A.M. a truck pulled up and we all loaded it with stoves, furniture, and other stuff that probably didn't even belong to her. After I had been around for a while I learned that restaurants that weren't making it often stole away in the middle of the night—just like packing your valise and leaving a hotel in the middle of the night without paying your bill. Another popular dodge is putting up a CLOSED FOR RENOVATION sign so the owners could get a head start before their landlord discovered that they were actually gone.

Not that Kyoto was always horrible to us; we were very well paid and she frequently took us out for expensive meals of Korean barbecue and sushi. Each time she took us out she said the same thing, like a little Japanese mother: "I don't expect anything in return. I just hope that some day some of you girls take me out for some sushi." She loved Emily; she called her muchacha and treated her as if she was her own child. After she left that Village space she opened a place in Chelsea and had an all-woman kitchen, made up mostly of all our friends who had been hired by Emily.

Kyoto also taught me the most important thing I ever learned about the restaurant business. I was always terrible in math and I never understood fractions. But once she explained the business in terms of money, suddenly I got it. Your restaurant, she said, is like a pie, and the more pieces that are taken out—for partners, for overhead, for food cost—the less there is in the business. The pie is in my head all the time.

When I nearly hacked through my thumb with a cleaver one night, putting myself in St. Vincent Hospital's emergency room, I took it as a sign and my career with Kyoto ended. In fact, I took it as a sign that I needed to leave New York for a while. A few months later I was in Maine beginning what I would look back on as the happiest time of my life.

Pearle's Gift

WE SAT EATING OUR LOBSTERS AT NUNAN'S IN EXHAUSTED SILENCE. My mother and I had dragged our best friends up to Kennebunk not to torture them, although as a matter of fact that is what the outcome was, but to have them help us move out of our house on Summer Street. After, we took them out for the best lobsters in Maine, to thank them for that day's work and fortify them for the rest of the weekend. We could have used some fortification ourselves and not of the lobster variety. We ate, took pictures at the table—which I cannot even bear to look at now, because the unhappiness is so evident on our faces—and generally tried to act like happy visitors. Somehow, even though our friends had spent time and effort, not to mention money to come up and help us, we could not rise to the occasion and be on our most respectful and grateful behavior. We had sold the home that Pearle "bought" and we were not happy.

Pearle at the Forest Hill House, circa 1932.

Pearle's death was an enormous loss for me, but the impression she made on me as a child, of a kind, hardworking, and elegant woman, was so complete that Pearle is always with me. Something unexpected came from her death too, and that is the home my mother bought in Kennebunk. Over the years Pearle had saved a nice sum of money, not in any investments of interest-bearing accounts but in about twelve low-interest passbook accounts. After the crash, I guess she figured better safe than sorry.

My mother knew exactly what she wanted to do with the money she inherited from Pearle. She wanted to buy a house in Maine, so one weekend in 1979 she got in the car, drove to Kennebunk, looked at a few houses, and bought one. The great thing about the Summer Street home was that we had a place to gather the family for the first time in years.

Summer Street was the only house I ever lived in with a history. I had grown up in what Pete Seeger called a ticky-tacky house in his song "Little Boxes." Don't get me wrong, there were woods and a reservoir behind it, and it was a great place to grow up. But the Maine house really felt like home.

"Has Anybody Seen This Garage?"

Summer Street remains a testament to the great wealth that sprang from the sea, and the incredible success of Kennebunk and Kennebunkport's seafaring community. Shipbuilders, captains, and merchants built enormous houses up and down Kennebunk's Summer Street, not far from the shipbuilding and launching hub of Kennebunk Landing. Captain Ivory Lord, master of his first ship at twenty-one, was the patriarch of a true seafaring family that extended to his children and sons-in-law. Co-owner with his brother of both a shipping and a shipbuilding company, he built his home in 1835 on Summer Street next door to and one year after his brother. In 1855, his son and heir, John Adams Lord, built an Italianate Victorian next door, complete with a tower and carriage house.

My mom bought John Adams Lord's house in 1979 and went to the Brickstore Museum to look into its history. When she heard the home originally came with a carriage house and that it had been moved, she wanted it back. So, she took a picture over to the *York County Coast Star* and put an advertisement in the paper: "Have you seen this house?" It was not such a far-fetched idea, since structures were often moved around "in the old days." Soon after, an old man called her one afternoon to say that he understood the garage had been rolled away to a neighboring street and had later burned down. Since she had her heart set on having the carriage house back and she had the original architect's drawings, she decided to have it replicated, on a slightly smaller scale. Her quest for the garage was subsequently chronicled in local architecture books.

Summer Folk

We had been *summer folk,* a term used by Kennebunkport natives to describe those *from away* who descend upon them each summer, opening summer homes or staying for months in the same familiar hotel. Summer folk, however, is a distinct and important upgrade from tourist, which sounds humiliating no matter what village in the world you are visiting but is somehow just a little more degrading in Maine.

Not that Mainers have anything against their summer visitors. On the contrary, since the late 1800s, the innkeepers and hoteliers of Maine have gone to great length to build the business of tourism and offer their guests the finest accommodations. Almost anything you could want from a vacation can be found there, especially if it has anything to do with being outdoors.

My grandmother, mother, and I had dreamed of living in Maine—or at least having a vacation home—and it had finally happened. But things weren't quite as my mother and I had expected. Renovating the house fell somewhere between the movies *Mr. Blandings Builds His Dream House* and *The Money Pit.* It was falling down around our ears and as soon as contractors realized we weren't locals, they began to circle. So I moved to Maine in the spring of 1980 and was upgraded to resident. But as a resident, Maine and I were immediately off to a questionable start.

Visiting the Kennebunks during the height of summer turned out to be considerably different than living there year-round. I oversaw much of the work on the house while my mother lived in Connecticut. During my first year there we had spring rains that went on for days. I came home late from work one night and thought I heard water running in the basement. When I went downstairs to investigate, I was aghast. Water was shooting out of the holes like it would out of a water pistol, with chunks of mortar flying from between the granite blocks. The water was inching up toward the boiler and I panicked. I had to figure out what to do to fix it, and as someone who had grown up in a modern house, I was at a loss. Luckily, I remembered that my mom had bought a wet/dry vac, so I ran the plug along the ceiling to avoid electrocution and spent the rest of the night vacuuming up the water and running the five-gallon bucket up to the kitchen to empty it into the sink.

The first few years, I closed off all of the rooms but the kitchen, dining room (which I used as a bedroom), and bathroom. I was making six or seven dollars an hour as a line cook and sous chef and frankly couldn't afford to heat a three-story home—sixteen rooms, plus a basement, tower, and attic. What heat I had came from a woodstove in the kitchen and a fireplace in the front sitting room. Wood was expensive for me, so I bought cords of wood in four-foot lengths and sawed them into chunks, then split the chunks and stacked it next to the kitchen.

A Family Reunites

David and his wife, Pippa, came to visit that first summer with their son Daniel. David was happy to be back in Kennebunkport and Pippa loved Maine, but little Daniel had some problems with beach etiquette.

One afternoon we were washing the sand off Daniel in the outdoor showers at the beach house when he slipped away. Typical two-year-old that he was, he took off like a shot and being fast and wet, he was particularly hard to catch. He happened to be naked and no sooner had we caught up with him than a very officious member of the club came over to scold the entire family. We were informed that no one, not even children, were allowed to go naked on the beach in front of the beach house. We tried to explain that an escaped, naked two-year-old had been more of an accident than an actual plan, but he was having none of it and walked away shaking his head at these people *from away*.

Kennebunkport was more than just a vacation for me, and, I think, my mother, and brother. Our family had been torn apart by divorce, my grandmother had died, and David had moved to Europe—continuity was completely missing from our family. For my mom, Gooch's Beach was

The fourth generation, David's son Daniel, playing in the surf at Gooch's Beach in the early 1980s.

a reminder of happy childhood memories and relatives that were long gone. When we went to the beach in the afternoons and sat in the same spot in front of the beach house that my grandparents did sixty years before, our little family suddenly didn't feel so fractured. Each summer for a few weeks, we were able to get together again and those memories, that feeling of family, carried us through until we were able to see each other again.

A Midsummer Shore Dinner

The summer that David, Pippa, and Daniel first came to visit was filled with beach food. We had shore dinners cooked in the big lobster pot that now hangs over the bar at Pearl Oyster Bar. Sometimes we would split the lobsters in half and throw them on the grill. We steamed clams and roasted dozens of ears of corn over the coals. We'd make salads of fresh lettuces and the ripest, sweetest tomatoes, or my mom would make her legendary Caesar salad. I have never eaten as many vegetables as I did during those summer and autumn seasons I lived in Maine.

It was while I was living in Kennebunk that I really learned how to use a grill. We didn't have air conditioning in our big old Victorian, and grilling outside kept the house from getting warmer during the summer and smelling like the docks for the rest of the night. Grilling was also the way to go when company visited. Preble Fish Company in Cape Porpoise was just a short ride away, so I would go pick out whatever seemed the freshest, bring it home, and marinate it in some fresh herbs and olive oil half an hour before I was going to cook it. When my guests arrived, I would fill everyone's glass and we would sit outside around the grill, visiting while the fish cooked. I roasted some sweet corn on the grill too, still in the husk and soaked with water so it wouldn't burn, and put a few new potatoes, rubbed with olive oil and wrapped in aluminum foil, deep in the coals to cook. To this day I use this simple, low-maintenance meal that doesn't take me away from my guests.

Behind the house there was a beautiful small yard with an acre of wild

Grilled Corn in the Husk

Put the corn, still in the husk, in your sink and soak it with cold water. If you're cooking the corn outside, put it on a medium fire for 10 to 12 minutes, turning frequently. You can also roast it in the oven at 450°F for 10 to 12 minutes.

Some chefs like to pull back the husk, peel off the silk, and then put the corn back in the husk. I prefer to leave it on because it keeps the corn moist. It may be a little harder to clean later, but it's worth it. When you're ready to serve, just shuck it, salt it, butter it, and eat it!

land beyond it, lavish with thousands of wild phlox, their sweet scent perfuming the night air. As the sky grew dark, Daniel would teeter around running after the fireflies, just like his grandmother had done fifty-five years before. That summer was lush and generous, just like all of those that have come after it. (Once I came to understand Maine winter, I found it almost as beautiful as summer.)

The times we enjoyed most at 32 Summer Street all revolved around food. Even if it was just my mom and me there, we would still make chowders and have mini-lobster bakes. There is nothing like the smoky, roasted taste of

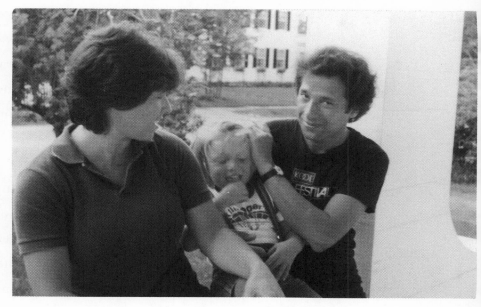

a lobster grilled outdoors in its shell, and if it's done properly, it stays juicy. As for clambakes, they are New England smorgasbords in a pot, with the best shellfish cooked in layers, between cobs of sweet corn and summer potatoes, all of the flavors seeping into one another. That's the thing about shore dinners and clambakes— they seem intimidating but are some of the easiest entertaining you can do. Whether you are in a two-room apartment in Manhattan, a beach house in Rhode Island, or a cabin in Maine, you can make these simple dinners work with the space and equipment you have.

Me with Daniel and David, on a visit to Summer Street in the early 80s.

Beach Classics

BEACH FOOD IS THAT GROUP OF VERY BASIC DISHES THAT CAN BE FOUND ON BOTH COASTS, MOST SHORES, AND THE BANKS OF OCEANS, RIVERS, AND LAKES. Although I consider what we serve at Pearl Maine or New England seafood, people have told me it reminds them of their beach experiences from Malibu to the chilly shores of Brighton in the United Kingdom. But we don't always get the best food we can at these clam and lobster shacks. We may remember it fondly, but that probably has more to do with being on vacation and near the beach than anything else.

Many times I have approached the counter of one place or another, excited to be ordering what I hope will be a fat, creamy lobster roll or a bucket of tender, juicy steamers only to be disappointed. When I started to make this food at Pearl, I was able to combine the simplicity of the dishes with the cooking techniques so sorely lacking in the fish shacks of coastal New England.

Steamers

Serves 2

In the late 1970s through the late 1980s, if you were in Portland, Maine, during happy hour, the place to be was J's Oyster Bar. After a long day on the water, fishermen, lobstermen, and everybody else packed into the tiny waterfront bar for some serious relaxation. J's had a unique gimmick to lure customers. Every hour a J's barmaid would ring an old nautical bell and the room would grow silent. She would pull a piece of paper from a man's hat that had the name of a common, everyday object on it, like a pocketknife. If you had whatever they called out, you got a free drink.

J's also served a limited menu of seafood and raw bar, including steamers that they would pile into banged-up tin buckets. I upscaled this for Pearl, and use shiny, stainless steel buckets on large platters, with ramekins of clarified butter and cups of broth on the side. But you can serve steamers in anything, so have some fun here. You can even serve it family style with the clams in a big bowl and give cups of broth and butter to each person.

1 to 2 pounds steamer clams per person
Drawn or clarified butter (page 62)
Italian parsley sprigs
Lemon wedges

The most important thing about cooking steamers is not the actual cooking process—it's securing the freshest, cleanest clams possible. Steamer clams come two ways, purged and unpurged. In wholesale markets unpurged clams cost considerably less than purged clams. Make sure you ask your fisherman which he's selling. At Pearl, we purge our own.

When purging the clams, you force them to spit out as much sand as possible so you don't end up spitting it out yourself. We accomplish this by adding cornmeal to the water the clams sit in, which irritates them and makes them release the sand. To purge them, put your clams in a container large enough to accommodate them. Pour in enough water to cover them. For every pound of clams, add $1/8$ cup cornmeal and mix it thoroughly into the water. The steamers need to purge for at least 3 or 4 hours; be sure to add a little ice from time to time to keep the clams cold. When the purging is complete (and you don't ever really know when that is), remove the clams from the bath and rinse them thoroughly in cold water. Refrigerate them until you are ready to use them.

To steam them, you can certainly use a steamer if you have one, but a large saucepan with a lid will do. Bring a cup of water per person to a boil, add the clams in a single layer, and cover them tightly. Steamers take about 3 to 4 minutes to cook—when they're open, they're ready. Discard any that are broken or that do not open.

Lift out the clams with a slotted spoon and arrange them in bowls. Pour off the broth into cups—there will be a little sand in the bottom, so take care not to pour everything out. Fill the ramekins with butter. Sprinkle the steamers with parsley sprigs, scatter the lemon wedges around the plate, and serve. Make sure you have bowls on hand for the empty shells.

The Proper Way to Eat a Steamer

There is a ritual to steamer eating. You need to take it out of the shell, grab the "dirty sock" (that's what we call it at Pearl, but it's really the membrane covering the tail), and pull it off, inside out just like you would a sock. Use the tail as a handle to dip it first in the broth, shaking it to remove any leftover sand. Then dip in the butter, put it in your mouth, and eat the whole thing. Most steamer aficionados drink the broth afterward. Be careful not to drink the last sip, though. It's sandy.

Deep Dirt on Clam Digging

A figure walks on the beach with the pale lemony yellow of an early sun, not quite up, glowing from behind with a funny old straw hat on, pant legs rolled up (clam diggers, of course), and an old bucket slapping rhythmically against one leg. Spying something, the figure stops, digs a toe into the damp, soft sand, bends, digs a small trowel into the mud, and pulls up a round, cool, gray clam. A small air bubble leads the figure to another, and another, until it seems like the clams are leaping up and sailing in an arc through the air, toward the rim of the bucket as if they are just begging to be caught. This is the romantic notion some of us have, or have had, about clam digging. The reality is not even close.

Clam digging takes effort, and why not? They are burrowing down into the sand for their lives, and they know it. They are going to make you work to get them. Clam digging is a wear-the-oldest-clothes-you-have-and-roll-up-your-sleeves kind of affair. There will be wet sand or mud in your hair, covering your clothes, and in your shoes. The muscles in your arms will tire from the digging and you will often be cold and uncomfortable in your pursuit. Of course, as bad as it is for you, think about the clam.

There are clamming regulations to be considered, too. Many states protect their clam crops by allowing clamming only at certain times of the year or limiting the amount you can take. Another really good reason to check with local marine or municipal officials before digging is that, in Maine, for instance, many mudflats are closed to clammers because of leaking septic tanks. Clams are suspension feeders, sucking phytoplankton down their siphon, but these siphons can accumulate toxins, causing illnesses as serious as hepatitis.

Armed with the important facts, you are ready to dig. First you must know your clam—are you going to be digging razor clams in Washington State or quahogs off Shelter Island? For our purposes, let's say we are digging for steamers, which are available up and down the Eastern Seaboard, generally plentiful, and as easy to prepare as boiling water.

Digging for Clams

1. **DON'T CROWD OTHER CLAMMERS;** should you see someone having a lot of luck, it doesn't mean you should hang your pail nearby. There are plenty to go around.

2. **FIND A STURDY SHOVEL, NOT TOO BIG, WITH A POINTED END.** You should be able to step on the edge and get into the sand fast and deep. You can also use a pitchfork. (I know one woman in Maine, as devoted a fisherman and clammer as you will ever know, who has used the same pail and pitchfork since she was a young girl.)

3. **BRING A GOOD-SIZED PAIL WITH YOU** that you can fill with enough water to cover your haul. This will keep them alive and fresh.

4. **LOW TIDE IS THE ONLY TIME TO DIG STEAMERS.** If you cannot figure it out, most areas have tide charts online now and you can plan ahead.

5. **WHERE TO DIG?** If you are vacationing in places like Kennebunkport or the Hamptons or North Fork of Long Island, where there are lots of choices from numerous beaches and coves to salt marshes, find someone who lives in the area and ask. Mainers, for instance, play it close to the vest, so chances are they will not tell you about the secret, special area they clam. But they will send you somewhere good enough to keep you from finding their spot!

6. **Look for tiny holes on the surface of the sand,** from $1/4$ to $1/2$ inch in diameter at the largest. The siphon, the tube that sticks out and is covered by the thin black membrane you pull off before eating, makes the holes.

7. **When you see the hole, turn your back to the water and dig** your shovel in about six inches or so behind it. Steamers are anywhere from three inches to a foot under the surface, so dig one neat, deep hole and set the shovel and sand aside. There is a whole world underneath that surface, so watch out for critters that fight back, like crabs. Their holes are bigger and tend to look like tunnels, which they are.

8. **The clams will be on red alert and ready to move now,** so you have to be, too! Quickly dig on the edges of the hole, using a little of the water that will start pouring into your hole to help ease them out. The clams should look like they are hanging there, suspended next to one another. Grab the ones that look like they can escape first. Any clam with a shell under two inches in length should be buried again in the sand.

9. **Once you get the hang of digging the clams, minimizing grit and sand is your main goal.** Take the clams in small batches and rinse them off well in the water before throwing them into the pail. This is also a good time to go through them. If you are out for a long time, change the water with some frequency.

Traditional Clambake

Serves 6 to 8

A TRADITIONAL CLAMBAKE REQUIRES MUSCLE, A BEACH WHERE THEY ALLOW COOKING, OR SOMEONE WILLING TO DONATE THEIR BACKYARD TO A TASTY CAUSE. Check your local beach's rules on open fires and cooking. There are some places that still allow it, but they are few. In some cases, for a large party or wedding, you can get a permit that will allow limited cooking for a day.

The Menu
Steamed lobsters
Steamer clams
Prince Edward Island mussels
New potatoes
Sweet corn

---

1 1^1/$_4$- to 1^1/$_2$-pound lobster per person

^{1}/$_2$ pound steamer clams per person

^{1}/$_2$ pound Prince Edward Island mussels per person, scrubbed and debearded

6 to 10 new medium potatoes

6 to 10 ears of sweet corn, husk on, soaked in water

1^1/$_2$ pounds melted butter, for dipping

Tools of the Trade:

A shovel

A tarp

Seaweed

Charcoal or wood, preferably a combination

Dig a deep pit, far away from anything flammable, in a yard or a beach. Put down a layer of coals and start a fire. Allow the coals to burn for an hour or more, until the entire area is hot. When the fire is ready, cover the coals with a thick layer of seaweed and begin to layer your food and fish on top. Foods that take longest to cook are put closer to the fire, working your way up to the foods that take the least amount of time to cook. So the order from bottom to top is: potatoes, corn, lobsters, clams, and steamers. Cover it all with more seaweed and then the tarp. It is impossible to say how long it will take to cook, since it depends on a number of variables. Play some beach volleyball or go for a swim, but keep checking under the tarp.

When it's all finished, I like to heap the mussels and clams into their own bowls, and then husk the corn and serve it on a big platter. I then give everyone a lobster, some potatoes, and a cup of butter for dipping and let them dig in. If you'd like, you can serve this with an heirloom tomato salad tossed with fresh herbs and dressed lightly wtih olive oil and vinegar.

You can also make this on a grill or on your stove, using a big stockpot and layering the food in the same way. Just put some water on the bottom to boil, and the steam will cook everything through.

Clam Fritters

Serves 4 to 6

1^1/$_2$ cups steamed chopped clams (about 12 quahogs)

1^1/$_2$ cups all-purpose flour

^{1}/$_2$ cup cornmeal

1 tablespoon baking powder

^{1}/$_4$ teaspoon kosher salt

^{1}/$_2$ teaspoon freshly ground black pepper

1 cup whole milk

^{1}/$_4$ cup clam juice

2 tablespoons (^{1}/$_4$ stick) butter, melted

3 eggs, lightly beaten

Vegetable, peanut, or canola oil

Steam open the clams (see page 149) and chop them roughly. In a large bowl, mix the flour, cornmeal, baking powder, salt, and pepper. Add the milk, ^{1}/$_4$ cup water, clam juice, and melted butter and mix until smooth. Add the eggs and clams and combine thoroughly. Allow the batter to rest at least an hour before using it.

In a deep saucepan or pot, heat roughly 2 to 3 inches of oil to 350°F. Dip a tablespoon into the oil to keep the batter from sticking to it. Drop a spoonful of batter into the hot oil, turning it after a minute or two until it's golden brown all over. Drain it on paper towels. Test the fritter to check for seasoning and adjust if necessary. Continue with the rest of the batter and serve the fritters immediately.

Variation: For corn fritters, substitute 1 cup cooked corn kernels for the clams. You can boil the ears or cook them in the husk, then slice off the kernels. Pulse them in the food processor until they're partially pureed. Omit the clam juice and replace with milk.

For a snazzy hors d'oeuvre, add small chunks of lobster to the batter.

Fried Oysters

Serves 2

6 to 8 medium oysters

Vegetable, peanut, or canola oil

1/2 cup cracker meal

1 1/2 cups flour

Kosher salt

Pearl Oyster Bar Tartar Sauce (recipe follows)

Greens and chives for garnish

Shuck the oysters and clean and save the shells. Place the oysters in a bowl in their liquor and refrigerate them until ready to fry. In a deep saucepan or pot, heat the oil to 350°F. Mix the cracker meal and flour in a large pie plate to make the dredge. Drain the oysters in a strainer and drop them into the dredge one by one, keeping them separated. Coat each oyster well, then shake off the excess dredge. Drop each oyster gently into the hot oil and fry until they are golden brown, about 3 to 4 minutes. It's important not to overfry them. Drain them on paper towels and sprinkle with kosher salt.

To serve, arrange the shells in a circle with the narrow ends of the shells in the center. Put a spoonful of tartar sauce in the center of each shell. Top it with a fried oyster. Garnish the plate with a bouquet of greens in the middle. I like to use a mixture of baby lettuces. Sprinkle it all with chives.

Pearl Oyster Bar Tartar Sauce

1/4 cup chopped red onion

1/4 cup roughly chopped capers

1/4 cup chopped cornichons, plus 2 tablespoons of the juice

3 cups Hellmann's mayonnaise

$1/2$ teaspoon kosher salt

$1/2$ teaspoon freshly ground black pepper

In a large bowl, mix the ingredients thoroughly. Refrigerate.

Fried Clams

Serves 4 as an appetizer

Ironically, even though making fried clams seems difficult, it's actually no more so than frying chicken, and these days it makes a lot more sense to make them at home. Clam shacks used to be cheap, no-frills places where you could get a quick meal for ten or fifteen bucks. Now, a quart of clams in a white paper carton with a couple of wooden forks sticking out and a few packages of tartar sauce costs nearly thirty dollars. Shucking clams is labor-intensive work, and these days it's tough to find that kind of manpower. When I buy shucked steamer clams for frying at the restaurant, they charge me more than $85 per gallon. The cheapest way to eat fried clams these days is to buy a few pounds of steamer clams, shuck them, and fry them up yourself.

To prepare them, just follow the fried oyster recipe on page 157 but substitute clams for the oysters.

Smackmen and Lobster Gangs

THE KEY TO THE MAINE ACCENT IS AN ALMOST MELODIC LILT. That's where most people go wrong when trying to mimic it; they make it too heavy and dull. But although Mainers do flatten out their vowels and soften "*r*'s" at the end of words, they are very gentle with their words. *Lobstuh* sounds better in Maine than anywhere else in the world.

The first time I went out on a fishing boat I was with my cousin Louise, and we just happened to be hung over. A fishing boat at dawn is not really where you want to be after a night of drinking with your cousin. But she was in town visiting and I thought she wanted to go and she thought I wanted to go, so off we went. About ten minutes into the trip we looked at each other and knew we were in trouble. The waves were pitching and rolling on a particularly rough sea and I quickly turned green. We sat in the stern for ninety minutes trying not to throw up until the captain finally decided to turn back because the seas were too rough.

Fisherman's boats on the beach.

Maine locals don't eat nearly as much lobster as someone *from away* might think. You would think that having lobsters so fresh that they're pulled right from the Gulf of Maine the same day you buy them available to you whenever you want would be irresistible. But the truth is, lobster has not always been considered the delicacy that we admire today.

In the old days lobster was so prevalent it was used, among other things, as fertilizer and food for prisoners. Somewhere in the early 1800s the lobster's reputation changed. High society in New York and Boston clamored for the succulent crustacean and the demand grew rapidly. Trap fishing didn't begin until roughly 1850, but in the early 1820s an important improvement happened in lobster fishing, which allowed Maine lobster to be bought and served outside of the state. Smackmen, named for the boat they used, were the first middlemen in the lobster industry. They played an invaluable role by buying lobsters from local fisherman and transporting them to metropolitan areas to sell. The key was the smack boat, which had a tank in the hull with holes drilled in it that allowed the saltwater to circulate and keep the lobsters alive and fresh. Of course, they tended to eat each other, as lobsters will do when they are cooped up together, especially if they haven't been given anything else to eat. When I first started cooking in the 1970s, lobsters came with little wooden pegs inserted in the claws between the thumb and the knuckle joint. Not only was this probably very painful but it was deemed unsanitary because the wood collected bacteria. Lobstermen have since replaced the pegs with thick, brightly colored rubber bands. The result was the same—lobster cannibalism.

Within a few years, smacks couldn't keep up with the popularity of lobster. Lobster had become a sign of wealth and restaurants were serving rich, flamboyant dishes like lobster Newburg and lobster thermidor. Other parts of the country, not just the places the smacks could reach, wanted Maine lobster too. When canneries came up with the idea of canning lobster meat, there was a small revolution. By the end of the 1800s, canned lobster was more expensive than live lobster. It was also harder to produce than it had been in the early days. Lobster life expectancy decreased enormously once the canning began. Since picking the meat is hard work, canneries in the 1800s wanted the larger four- and five-pound lobsters, but they were reduced to picking lobsters as small as half a pound. This was obviously before regulations on lobster size were instituted. "Shorts" are less than one pound and must be thrown back into the water to mature. Female egg-bearing lobsters are also supposed to be thrown back, although I do get those at the restaurant on occasion and it always makes me terribly sad. For of the thousands of the eggs she carries, only a few live to be full-grown lobsters.

Lobster Gangs

If you think you're going to go up to Maine and throw your own lobster pots into the water, think again. Every inch of good—and not so good, for that matter—lobstering and fishing water is spoken for. Maine's fishing community is tight, whether it's scallops, shrimp, haddock, sea urchins, groundfish, cod, or lobsters being fished. Anthropologists have nicknamed these groups lobster gangs, a nickname that denotes their loyalty and honor. Men who all fish from the same harbor come to rely on and respect each other, whether or not they may socialize off the docks. The best fishermen are called highliners, and therefore sit at the top of the hierarchy. There are regulations and laws designed to protect local fishermen, some of whom are the tenth or eleventh generation in their family to fish these waters. Almost nine thousand people have lobstering licenses, and Maine's yearly lobster catch is about 46 million pounds. It may sound like a lot, but at my little restaurant that's open six days a week, I use two hundred pounds per day—more than thirty tons per year. New fishermen have to go through channels to be assigned a fishing territory within a harbor. While rules for the lobstering community are not written anywhere, there is a code that you are expected to observe.

Most lobster fishermen beat the sunrise and are in their boats by 5:30 A.M. In the early morning a light fog may cover the port as they pull out, but the seas are calmer and the heat is still manageable. By afternoon the swells are more likely to rock the boat, making hauling traps from the depths of the sea much harder. The fisherman usually works with one stern man, who gets paid by a percentage of the haul. They bring lunch and a supply of water with them, motoring out miles from the coast to their territory where their pots have been dropped. Each harvester has his own territory, some passed down through the generations, marked by buoys in his color pattern. It is an honor system, and no fisherman would dare touch another harvester's traps. The team works all day, pulling in around three hundred traps. They handle each lobster, checking it for size and making sure it's not a female carrying eggs. Then the claws of the ones being kept are banded, and the lobsters are thrown in a saltwater tank. The traps are then rebaited, reset, and sent back down.

Fisherman's Festival

If you're up for an early spring trip Down East, there is a beloved festival that has taken place in Boothbay Harbor annually for thirty years. The Fisherman's Festival takes place each year at the end of April as the new fishing and lobstering season is about to get under way. It begins with the Miss Shrimp Princess pageant on Friday night and culminates on Sunday afternoon with a service at the fishermen's memorial in honor of local men who have died at sea. The Blessing of the Fleet follows, commercial fishing vessels gathering in the harbor and circling the memorial one by one to receive the clergyman's blessing for a safe and profitable year.

Events for competing fishermen include lobster crate running, which tests agility by having the participant run over the tops of lobster crates tethered together and strung between two docks. There is also the dory bailing contest, where teams of three see who can bail out their boat first, and a trap hauling contest, which is really a race. The boat captain and stern man run from the top of the dock to their boat, untie it and race out to traps set in the inner harbor, haul, bait, reset the traps, race back to the dock, retie the boat, and run back up the ramp.

No festival is complete without lots of food, such as the pancake breakfast at the Congregational Church, the fish fry at the Boothbay region lobsterman's co-op, or the church supper, and after you've eaten, you can check out the dockside dance on Saturday evening. For those landlubbers with the heart of a fisherman, there is an evening event called "Tall Tales" at a local bar, where fishermen pull out their best stories. There are also lighthouse tours, and scallop- and oyster-shucking contests. One of the best things about going to Maine this time of the year, other than minimal invasion by other tourists, is watching winter release its snowy hold to make room for a beautiful spring.

Lobster festivals are held all over the state throughout summer. But the granddaddy of them all is the Maine Lobster Festival held each year midcoast, in Rockland. For five days in late July and early August, you can gorge yourself on steamed lobster from the world's largest lobster cooker, corn on the cob, steamed and fried clams, fried Maine shrimp, shrimp cocktail, and steamed mussels in wine and vegetable sauce. Amateur cooks can enter the Maine seafood cooking contest while the rest of the family goes off to watch the crowning of Miss Sea Goddess or one of the many concerts and competitions. Rockland is one of Maine's art centers, home to the Farnsworth Museum, which holds the main gallery for Monhegan Island resident Andrew Wyeth, his father, N. C., and son Jamie. So the lobster festival itself has a note of culture, with photography and art exhibits, and a juried art show.

<hr>

It's a long, hard day with a high overhead. I've stood on the harbor watching the lobstering boats pull in to Cape Porpoise when the sun is low in the sky, making the water shimmer. The captain is at the helm in his bright orange rubber overalls and boots, brown as a horse chestnut from being on the water all day and thoroughly exhausted. In this disposable age the lobsterman repairs his broken traps, since they can cost as much as eighty dollars each. If a storm wipes out his traps, it can cost him more than sixty thousand dollars, because lobstering equipment is considered a bad risk and too vulnerable to be covered by insurance. Fuel and bait range from one to two hundred dollars per day and maintenance is yet another expense. The boat itself can cost a couple of thousand for a rowboat or a couple of hundred thousand for an inboard with diesel power. So, while you won't be becoming a lobster harvester anytime soon, Maine is a paradise for sport fishing with its array of waterways and fish.

There are hundreds of qualified guides willing to take you anywhere the fish run, from deep sea fishing in the Atlantic to tiny secret fishing spots and fish camps along the lakes, rivers, and streams. Trout, bass, and landlocked salmon flourish in the freshwater bodies of Maine. If you're looking for the familiar silver Atlantic salmon, the salmon we buy in grocery stores and fish markets, the only rivers in which you'll find it in the United States are in Maine. Highly coveted bluefish are found in Maine's tidal rivers; haddock and cod are still fished here too, though both have been near tragically over-fished. The lobstering community is well aware of the mistakes made in over-fishing through the years and protects their future fiercely. "Maine" lobsters are found from North Carolina to New Brunswick, Canada, but Maine is the only state that doesn't drag the ocean floor for their catch. They have, as all good fishermen have, become ecologists able to make their living from the water while also protecting it.

We eat so much more fish now that we are going to find many species in jeopardy if we're not careful. All fishing should model lobstering, which max-imizes the catch while taking vigilant care to insure the lobster's future. At Pearl, nothing seems to make customers happier than to eat lobster, whether it's in a lobster chef salad, a lobster roll, or a "plain old" boiled or grilled shore dinner. Eating lobster always feel like a luxury, like you're pampering yourself. In the spring, early summer, and fall, you can get some good prices on lobster in your local grocery store, so treat yourself and bring a couple home to make your own shore dinner. Just remember to pick the liveliest ones in the tank, and don't let them sit around too long before cooking them. A rule of thumb—and my motto, one of them anyway—is never cook a dead lobster. Cook them, then pick the meat. You can refrigerate it for a day or two. Also remember that lobsters have a knack of moving pretty quickly, even when they have their claws banded.

My friends Robin Green and Mitch Burgess and I were doing a shoot for *New York* magazine with an "urban clambake" theme. Robin, who with partner

Mitch is an executive producer for *The Sopranos,* talked a friend into letting food editor Gillian Duffy at *New York* magazine use their backyard for the shoot and their downstairs kitchen to prep the food. Several days later the good-natured Gillian called me to say that the homeowner had to have his living room professionally cleaned and would be sending the bill to the magazine. For nearly a week they had smelled something increasingly foul in the house. Frustrated, he went on an inch-by-inch search of his house to find out what was causing this stench, when he turned up one of our lobsters. Seems when no one was looking it had gotten out of the bag, jumped (or more likely fell) down off the counter, crawled down a long hall turning a corner, to finally settle down under a stuffed chair in the living room and die.

Urban Clambake

Anyone can have a clambake; you don't have to be on the beach. I developed this version of a clambake for *New York* magazine. The idea was to deconstruct the traditional clambake, replacing traditional elements with more sophisticated recipes.

The Menu

Scallop Chowder with Pernod and Thyme (page 13)

Split Grilled Lobsters with Herb Butter Sauce (page 173)

Blueberry Bread Pudding with Vanilla
Custard Sauce (page 110)

LOBSTER
Lobster Picking

First of all, it is nearly impossible to get raw lobster meat out of the shell. If you manage, it is because you have virtually torn it out, so it won't be in very good shape. If you must, you can buy cooked lobster meat in most grocery stores now, though it will cost you more. Some stores will even cook your lobsters for you right on the spot.

If your recipe calls for picked lobster meat, boil the lobster as you would if you were making a boiled lobster dinner. I like to use 1 to $1^1/2$-pound lobster culls (lobsters with one or no claws, which tend to be less expensive) because there is no sense in spending money on a good-looking lobster when all you want is its meat. The culls will take from 7 to 10 minutes to cook and will float when done. Submerge in an ice bath to stop the cooking, then drain.

Separate the tail and claw from the body. You can throw the body away, or use it to make Lobster Stock (see page 174). Using a towel, lightly crush the tail with the heel of your hand to crack the shell. Bend the sides of the shell back and remove the tail in one piece. Separate the claw from the elbow (or knuckle) by holding the claw in your hand and pressing against the knuckle hard on a flat surface. Hold the claw in one hand and whack the top with the back of a chef's knife, giving the blade a little twist at the end. If you do this right, it will separate the shell into two pieces. Wiggle the thumb part back and forth and pull it off. If you're lucky and careful, the thumb meat will remain attached. Pull the claw meat out. With the small end of a fork or spoon, pry the meat out of the upper portion of the knuckle. Put the spoon end in again and break off that piece of empty shell. Now pry the meat out of the remaining piece of shell. Cut the tail in half lengthwise, then into $3/4$-inch chunks. Pull the claw meat apart with your fingers, because there is cartilage in the claws that needs to be removed.

Sea Bass Fillet with Lobster Broth and Aromatic Vegetables

Serves 4

2 carrots, peeled

1 large zucchini, seeded

2 large leeks, white part only

16 whole mushrooms, shiitake, oyster, or miatake or any combination

3 tablespoons unsalted butter (1 tablespoon may be truffle butter)

Kosher salt and freshly ground black pepper

4 cups Lobster Stock (page 174)

1 tablespoon olive oil

4 6- to 8-ounce black sea bass fillets, with the skin scored

Chopped chives for garnish

Preheat the oven to 450°F.

Julienne the carrots and zucchini on a mandoline and the leeks by hand, making a sort of vegetable spaghetti. (All the vegetables can be done by hand, of course.) In a sauté pan, sauté the mushrooms in 1 tablespoon of butter over medium heat until lightly browned. Set them aside, wipe out the pan, and melt another tablespoon of butter over medium heat. Sauté the carrots for about 1 minute. Add the leeks and sauté for another 2 minutes. Now add the zucchini and sauté for about 2 minutes. Season the vegetables with salt and pepper. Add the mushrooms and the lobster stock and bring to a simmer. Check the seasoning, bring up the salt, and add a little black pepper if necessary. At this point, for a little richer broth, you can swirl in a tablespoon of truffle butter or unsalted butter.

In a large sauté pan over medium-high heat, add the oil. Just before it reaches the smoking point (you may see a wisp or two of smoke but you never want it to be hot enough that it is smoking a lot), lay the fillets in the pan carefully, skin-side down. Shake the pan to make sure they don't stick. Sear the skin for about 2 minutes. When it gets lightly brown around the edges, finish it in the oven for about 3 to 4 minutes, or until the meat is pure white with no opacity.

Serve the fish in large shallow soup bowls. Lift out the vegetables and split them among the bowls, then lay the fish on top, skin-side up. Arrange the mushrooms around the bowls. Pour in the broth. Sprinkle with chives.

Lobster Chef Salad with Basil Vinaigrette

Serves 2

This is a composed salad, which means it should look picturesque when you are finished arranging it on the plate. I like to group things together using the prettiest vegetables available. Use a variety of tomatoes in different colors, such as pear, cherry, heirloom, and vine-ripened.

Although this is a recipe for 2 people, it can also serve 4 to 6 people as a side salad; just serve it on a large platter.

12 small wax beans

12 haricots verts

3 hard-boiled eggs, chopped

4 slices crisp-cooked country or double-smoked bacon
    (although regular bacon will do)

4 tomatoes, chopped

1 endive, chopped

1 ripe avocado, peeled, seeded, and chopped

8 white or red creamer potatoes, cooked and chopped

3 to 4 leaves each Boston, Bibb, lolla rosa, and red oakleaf lettuces,
    washed and spun dry

Meat from 2 $1^1/2$-pound lobsters, cooked, picked, and chilled
    (see picking directions on page 166)

Basil vinaigrette (recipe follows)

In a small saucepan over medium-high heat, boil or steam the beans, then plunge them immediately into an ice water bath to cool them and preserve the color. Arrange all of the ingredients on a plate, with the lobster meat in the center, and serve it with the basil vinaigrette on the side.

Basil Vinaigrette

3/4 cup pure olive oil (not extra-virgin)

1/4 cup white wine vinegar

1 tablespoon sherry vinegar

1 tablespoon chopped fresh basil

Kosher salt and freshly ground black pepper

In the bowl of a food processor or by hand, slowly combine the oil and the vinegars. Add the basil and season to taste with salt and pepper.

Pearl Oyster Bar Lobster Potpie

Serves 4

You can serve this pie the old-fashioned way, in one large soufflé or casserole dish, or in small, individual soufflé dishes or ramekins, about 4 inches deep and 5 inches wide. They are pretty easy to find and don't cost very much.

3 tablespoons unsalted butter

16 shiitake mushrooms, stemmed (julienne any caps that are larger than the size of a quarter)

10 cremini mushrooms, quartered

Pinch of kosher salt

4 shallots, chopped

1 cup amontillado sherry

1/2 cup Lobster Stock (page 174), optional

5 1/2 cups heavy cream

1 cup potatoes (any white potato will do), cut into 1/4-inch dice

$^1/_2$ cup carrots, cut into $^1/_4$-inch dice

1 cup fresh peas, shelled (or snap peas, bias cut into $^1/_4$-inch pieces)

Freshly ground black pepper

2 tablespoons truffle butter (optional)

Pastry dough (see Note)

Meat from 4 1-pound lobsters, cooked and picked
   (1 tail and 1 claw per person)

Egg wash

In a large sauté pan or pot, melt 2 tablespoons butter over medium heat. Add the shiitake and cremini mushrooms and a pinch of salt, and sauté them slowly until they are lightly browned, about 4 minutes. Place them in a bowl and set aside. Add the remaining 1 tablespoon butter to the pan and sauté the shallots over low heat until they are translucent, about 4 minutes. Return the mushrooms to the pan and deglaze the pan with the sherry. Add the stock if you want a slightly fuller-bodied sauce.

Raise the heat to medium and reduce the sauce to roughly 3 table-spoons. Add the cream and potatoes and simmer for 1 minute. Add the carrots and peas and reduce the sauce by one third, about 3 to 4 minutes. Season to taste with salt and pepper. Remove the pan from the heat and swirl in the truffle butter, if using.

Preheat the oven to 425°F. Roll out the pastry dough and, using a soufflé dish as a pattern, cut the pastry around the dish with a paring knife, leaving an extra $^1/_4$ inch for shrinkage. On a cookie sheet, lay out the pastry rounds and make steam vents in the tops so that the steam can escape when it's on top of the potpie during cooking. If you like, you can decorate the tops by cutting shapes out of the leftover dough with a cook-ie cutter. I like to use fish shapes. Bake the crust for 8 minutes, or until it is slightly browned.

Put a generous amount of lobster meat in each dish. Ladle the vegetables and sauce on top, leaving about a $^1/_2$ inch from the top. Top it with the pastry. Brush the pastry with the egg wash and finish it in the oven for 5 minutes, or until the filling starts to bubble.

Note: To make the pastry dough, follow the instructions for the crust portion of Blueberry Crumble Pie, page 108.

Lobster Stew

Serves 2

1 1$^1/_2$-pound live lobster

1 tablespoon oil

Kosher salt and freshly ground black pepper

$^1/_2$ cup amontillado sherry

1 tablespoon unsalted butter

4 white mushrooms, stems trimmed, quartered

$^3/_4$ cup Lobster Stock (page 174)

1 parsnip, peeled and cut into $^1/_2$-inch dice

1 carrot, peeled and cut into $^1/_2$-inch dice

1 large potato, cut into 1-inch dice

$^1/_2$ cup peas

1 cup heavy cream

$^1/_2$ teaspoon chopped flat-leaf parsley

$^1/_2$ teaspoon chopped chives

To prepare the lobster, use the point of a sharp chef's knife to make an incision behind the lobster's eyes, pushing straight down through to the board. Then bring the knife down, cutting between the eyes. Cut the lobster in half lengthwise. Cut the halved tail pieces in half. Remove the claw/knuckle section from the body. Crack the claws with the back of a chef's knife and crack the knuckle section. Reserve the body for lobster stock.

In a hot 10-inch skillet, add the oil. Lightly season the lobster pieces with salt and pepper and add them to the pan, sautéing 3 minutes on each side until red. Deglaze the pan with $1/2$ cup of the amontillado sherry. Pour the lobster and liquid into a bowl and reserve, keeping warm. Wipe out the pan. Over medium heat, add the butter and sauté the mushrooms until they brown a little, about 4 minutes. Deglaze the pan again with the remaining $1/4$ cup sherry. Add the lobster stock, the rest of the vegetables, and a sprinkle of salt, and sauté for 4 minutes. Add the cream and simmer it for 5 more minutes, until the vegetables are tender when pierced. Return the lobster to the pan. Season with salt and pepper and finish with the parsley and chives. Serve the stew immediately with crusty bread or oyster or common crackers.

Split Grilled Lobsters with Herb Butter Sauce

Serves 4

As a side dish, serve the Sweet Corn Ragout (page 69).

1 pound sweet butter

$1/2$ teaspoon chopped fresh tarragon

$1/2$ teaspoon chopped Italian parsley

$1/2$ teaspoon chopped chives

4 $1^{1}/2$-pound live lobsters

1 tablespoon olive oil

Kosher salt and freshly ground black pepper

2 large lemons, cut into sixths

To clarify the butter, in a medium saucepan over very low heat, melt the butter. Turn off the heat and pour off the golden butter, leaving the milk solids behind. Keep the clarified butter in a warm place until you're ready to use it. (You can prepare the butter ahead of time and store it in the refrigerator until you need it. Just bring it to room temperature.) When you're ready to grill the lobster, mix the tarragon, parsley, and chives into the butter.

Preheat the grill to medium-high heat. To prepare the lobster for grilling, make an incision with the point of a sharp chef's knife behind the lobster's eyes, pushing straight down through to the board. Then bring the knife down, cutting between the eyes. Turn the lobster around and finish cutting it down through the body and tail—you may need both hands to make sure it's completely cut through. Drizzle the lobster with a little olive oil and season it with salt and pepper. Place the lobsters on the grill, shell-side down. They will cook completely on this side; do not turn them over or you will lose precious juices. The lobsters will take about 7 to 10 minutes to cook; they are done when the meat is firm, with no translucency. Keep in mind that the tails cook faster than the claws, so move them around as needed to ensure even cooking. Baste them with the herbed butter a couple of times during grilling.

Serve the lobsters on individual platters with ramekins of herbed butter and plenty of lemon.

Lobster Stock

At the restaurant, we don't cavalierly toss out lobster bodies. When we make bouillabaisse, we freeze the raw bodies. And after we pick the meat for our lobster rolls we keep the cooked bodies for stock. Lobster stock is a wonderful addition to any kitchen and is really underutilized. It's richer than plain fish stock and has a more vibrant color. It's a terrific addition to dishes that call for stock. Virtually fat-free, lobster stock can be a flavorful way to cut down on fat and calories and is wonderful for making risotto, soups, and pastas. When customers at my restaurant want mussels but don't want the mustard cream sauce I serve, I reduce some lobster stock, add chopped leeks and fennel, season it, and steam the mussels in it.

Remember that whenever you cook lobsters at home, it's always smart to save the carcasses in the freezer for future stock, just as you might a roasted chicken carcass. When you accumulate enough, you can make a large pot of stock and keep it in containers in the freezer for easy access.

3 to 4 pounds raw or cooked lobster bodies

3 or 4 tablespoons vegetable, peanut, or canola oil

1 large onion, chopped

2 celery ribs, chopped

2 carrots, peeled and chopped

2 parsnips, peeled and chopped

2 whole heads of garlic, halved

1/2 bulb of fennel, sliced and cored

2 saffron threads

1/2 small bunch parsley

3 to 4 whole thyme stalks

1 13-ounce can whole tomatoes with juice, crushed

2 cups white wine

If you are using raw lobster bodies, in a large sauté pan over high heat, sauté the bodies, chopped claws, and tail in 1 tablespoon of oil with the onion, celery, carrots, parsnips, garlic, and fennel until the vegetables take on a little color; this will take about 10 minutes. Or, you can roast the mixture at 400°F until it's browned. Personally, I find this method easier, because it saves you a lot of stirring and watching. If you are using the cooked lobster carcass from a previous lobster dinner, roast only the vegetables and add lobster to the stockpot later with the rest of the ingredients. Remember that the stock won't have as rich a flavor as one made with raw lobster bodies.

Whether you are using cooked or live lobster, remember to remove the head sack and its contents.

Transfer the lobster and vegetables to a large stockpot. Add the saffron, parsley, and thyme, tomatoes, and wine and fill the pot with 3 quarts of water. Bring it to a boil, then turn it down to a simmer. Let it simmer for 1 to $1^{1}/4$ hours. Put the stock through a fine strainer, discard the solids, and cool. Use the stock within a couple of days or freeze for future use.

Red Dogs and Whoopie Pies

AS SOMEONE USED TO EATING—NOT TO MENTION COOKING—IN NEW YORK CITY, THERE WAS MUCH THAT I MISSED IN MAINE. Dinner out was oversauced, overcooked fish or meat with limp gray vegetables and salads that consisted of a wedge of iceberg lettuce, a few crescents of mealy tomatoes, and a clump of gooey "blue cheese" or French dressing.

In summer things improved significantly. Hard-working local farms kept us knee-deep in herbs and vegetables—just the basics but they were fresh. Fishermen worked the waters, supplying us with fish of all kinds. But the cornucopia of late spring, summer, and early fall was empty by late September. I was from New York, and used to buying arugula in the dead of winter. Here the only green thing one could get from October through June was iceberg lettuce. Since I

Atlantic Hall in Cape Porpoise, Maine.

wasn't much of a chef when I went up there, it wasn't that I was being creatively stunted or anything by the complete lack of variety. It just took me longer to acclimate to the food than anything else.

I can sum it up with a description of two items that are forever embedded in my memory: bright red hot dogs and bread so mushy that the word *crust* could only be used as a technical term for the slightly less spongy edge of the slice. Now when I say red hot dogs, I don't mean "red hot" red like a baseball park frank. These dogs, which you can still find in Maine grocery stores, have an almost Day-Glo pink casing that snaps when you bite into it. As for bread, there wasn't so much as an inch of the flaxen shivery crust we know so well today. The bread would trick me sometimes too. I'd go into a bakery or a store and see what looked like a crunchy, toasty loaf, only to bring it home and discover it was really just soft bread masquerading as a crusty loaf.

Maine had some exceptions, such as the whoopie pie (two round, chocolate cake–like cookies filled with a thick layer of cream) and Flo's Hot Dogs on Route 1 in Cape Neddick, a local food landmark, but a tough room to "work." Long before Seinfeld's Soup Nazi, Flo was making great dogs—with plenty of attitude—at her little roadside shack. She was packed from morning to dinnertime, despite a décor that consisted mainly of business cards from around the country thumbtacked to the walls and a limited menu. By limited menu, I mean that Flo served hot dogs and sodas and that was it. The hot dogs came "with everything"—onions, chili, mustard, relish, ketchup, and mayonnaise—unless you were brave or foolish enough to ask for just mustard or something else. Then your hot dogs came with a sneer or worse, and she remembered this slight the next time you came in.

Cooking at home could be even more depressing, because I had to rely on grocery stores. Actually it would be more appropriate to say "grocery store," because for the first few years I lived in the Kennebunks, there was only one tiny Shop 'n Save serving the entire area. Other stores like Bradbury's in Cape Porpoise were wonderful, old-fashioned grocers, but they sold only the staples and were really more like meeting places that housed the post office and notary. I'll never forget the overwhelming joy I felt in the late1980s when Shop 'n Save opened the kind of big, boxy grocery stores with shelves and shelves of products that I was used to. My cooking friends Mark, Evalin, and I reminisce about it to this day.

Not only were the stores and food lacking, but things like signs were confusing. When I first moved to Maine, my mom and I drove down the roads constantly perplexed. When you entered Maine from New Hampshire you drove over the Piscataqua Bridge. It took us a while to figure out how to pronounce that one, but not nearly as long as figuring out the meaning of NAT BUT SUG. All summer we would drive around and see signs advertising NAT BUT SUG. We couldn't figure out what in the world they were talking about. We still wouldn't know if I hadn't seen a sign that had enough room to spell out the phrase: native butter-and-sugar corn.

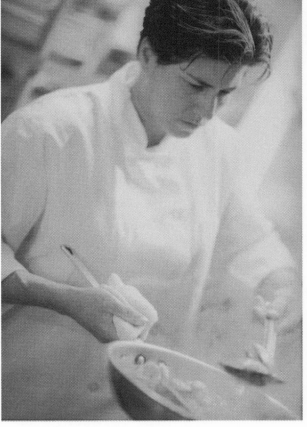

Becoming a Chef

The year my mom bought the house in Kennebunk coincided with the year I didn't really know what to do with myself. By accident I had been making my living as a cook, but I still wasn't sure what I wanted to do for a living.

Me at home in the kitchen at Pearl.

Since childhood I had watched my grandmother and mom in the kitchen. Growing up in the 1950s, with a mom who worked and drove us to lessons and appointments, we had our share of Stouffer's and quickie casseroles. But both my mother and Pearle took great pride in the meals they created. We had roast goose on holidays and hors d'oeuvres at cocktail hour. It wasn't just the food but the ritual that captivated me as a child and made the greatest impression on me. I remember the perfect blue Spode platter under my grandmother's roast goose and her staggering array of silverware—when my mom presented it to me recently, we went through it and many of the pieces *still* confounded us. I may not have grown up cooking at their elbows but my grandmother and my mom were nevertheless the great food influences on my youth.

Transplanted to Kennebunkport, I was once again faced with finding a job. As thoroughly as possible, without really having anyone to ask, I did a little nosing around to find out which were the better restaurants—there were certainly no great ones. The only two worth their salt were the Whistling Oyster, headed by chef Michael Allen, and Arrows. Allen had been hired away from Boston, where he had cooked with the legendary Madeleine Kamman at her Cambridge restaurant.

When I applied to him for a job, Michael hired me for the only position he had open at the time, garde-manger—the station that produces salads, first courses, and desserts. Although I had been a line cook for a while and had even been a chef at two restaurants, I decided to take the job. I realized I knew nothing—I had been faking it. Michael knew more and had more background than anybody I had ever worked with. I knew I could learn a lot from him.

Now, I have always maintained that women are better at garde-manger than men. As sexist and strange as this sounds, I think it's in part because of our smaller hands. But also it's been my experience that most men are not interested in the arranging of the delicate lettuces, slivers of vegetables, little pieces of fruit, and the minute details that make up the presentation of a composed plate. Guys like to flash around the hot line, banging their tongs as the flames shoot up and lick the back of the hood—most of them would skip garde-manger altogether if they could. I think this is a huge mistake because while they will learn how to cook the food, they will never understand how to present it well. Presentation is about symmetry, asymmetry, texture, balance, color, and a host of other elements that can be learned only in garde-manger.

Michael Allen was an exception. He understood that the food that came out of the garde-manger station was the foundation for a good menu. His recipes for vinaigrettes, purées, and emulsions were advanced and unconventional. In 1981, he served a cold veal tenderloin salad with grapes, a grape Cognac vinaigrette, and a radish mignonette for oysters that were inspired. There were also wonderful composed salads like lobster with Persian melon, papaya, mint, and a mango vinaigrette.

Working for Michael was a turning point for my career. He was so excited about food, and he wanted the people who worked for him to feel the same way—it was infectious. I had a lot to learn, but for the first time I knew what I wanted to do and I really felt like I was beginning to understand the mystery of how to make food taste good. For almost three years I worked there, moving up from garde-manger, to fish station, to meats. The Whistling Oyster was the culinary school I never had. Not only did I find my career, but I made some lifelong friends.

When Michael finally became so frustrated with the owners' insistence on trying to control the menu and just couldn't take it anymore, he went back to Boston. In the kitchen, we were heartbroken to see him go—we were like a rudderless ship at that point. My best friend Mark Gaier took over as chef and I became sous chef. If Michael hadn't left, however, it would have taken Mark and I a lot longer to find our legs as chefs. After all, if you don't take jobs that are over your head, then you won't advance.

Sometimes you just find a soul mate in life, and Mark was that for me. We were a little too inexperienced for our jobs, but we just kept making Michael's recipes, doing the best we could, and as far as I can tell, we got away with it. Mostly, we had a lot of fun.

The kitchen was filled with characters at that point. Evalin Stearns, a wraith of a woman with the shattering voice of a hog caller, came in to take my place in garde-manger. We gave her the nickname Belon, after the European oyster that had immigrated to Damariscotta, because that's all she ended up doing—shucking those thin, incredibly hard-to-open oysters. Evalin was energetic and added a certain urgency to the mix.

There's always somebody who flares around the kitchen so fast they don't think and are therefore prone to extravagant near misses. In our kitchen that was Paul "Flare" Connor, who buzzed around the stove on busy nights, pans clanking and food flying. But he always knew how to make us laugh by doing things like stuffing kiwi slices behind the lenses of his round glasses and impersonating Little Orphan Annie. Ron Siegel, on the other hand, with his unflappable demeanor was perfect for the line. Nothing bothered him, regardless of how many slips were on the board or how many mistakes the people around him were making. Thia, then his girlfriend and now his wife, rounded out the raucous group working in garde-manger when Belon was off.

We didn't have Prohibition like in my grandmother's day, but everything shut down early on the southern coast of Maine. We bolted out of work, moving rapidly through local bars, such as the Old Village Inn, the Front Porch, or Dune Lawn, until they closed at one in the morning. We stayed out especially late on Saturday nights, often ending up at one of our houses for a party. This was particularly stupid because Sunday was the only morning we served brunch. We'd come in so hung over that the only way we could get through it was with a hair of the dog, as it were.

Now, you couldn't get into the bar because the owners were no fools and kept it locked up. But we did have the bakeshop tucked behind the line with a floor-sized Hobart mixer, double convection oven, and shelves lined with our baker's cookbooks and liqueurs. Fortunately she used Cognac in the mousse, because I for one could not have withstood Grand Marnier, Midori, or Kahlúa when hung over. The whole operation was very covert, and to her credit, the baker never mentioned her disappearing Cognac. She just ordered more. To hide the actual drinking, Mark and I took to pouring the Cognac into little portion cups or, as we came to call them, "potion" cups. Every kitchen uses them, sometimes to serve dressings on the side or for things like the melted butter that accompanies lobster. Ours were paper lined with foil so we could bake in them. As it happened, they made a much better "shot glass" that way too. When we were occasionally forced to use paper, we noticed the Cognac ate right through them, and probably our stomachs, as empty as they were on Sunday mornings. One of us would call out "potion" and everyone would scurry behind the line, fill up a potion cup, and take it back to his or her station.

As much fun as it is, the kitchen can also be an amazingly dangerous place. One Sunday morning following a particularly festive Saturday night, I woke up and decided to go in early to set up for brunch service. (In truth, I was probably still a little tipsy.) No one else was there, so I decided to set up a few stations. When I went to start the burner, I waited just a little too long between turning on the gas and lighting the match. Whoosh! The flames shot up, removing my bangs, eyebrows, and eyelashes for several months. I couldn't see a thing. By the time Mark found me, I had managed to grope my way out of the kitchen and onto the back steps. He now tells me, "You were just whimpering and shaking on those back steps saying, 'I'm blind. I'm blind.' It's funny now because you got your sight back in a few minutes, but it was terrifying then."

Kitchens are hot, especially in summer, and we were prone to taking nearly naked group sponge baths in the walk-in. On an eighty-degree night, a kitchen with twelve burners, a fryer, a grill, a flat top, and a steam table is usually well over one hundred degrees (at Arcadia, we put a thermometer next to the stove and it regularly read 118 degrees). There are very few ways to cool off. Mark and I and the other line cooks used to go down to the walk-in refrigerator with wet kitchen towels, strip down, and give ourselves sponge baths whenever we got the chance.

All Grown Up

You would think we all would have ended up in a sanatorium somewhere, but each of us in our way managed to find our way in the food industry. The line became a little too much for "Flare," who switched to the calmer, more solitary pursuit of pastry chef and who my radar last tracked to the kitchen of a well-known Boston chef. Pastry chefs come in early in the morning when no one else is around, forcing them to spend too much time alone. Pastry is a very exacting science, and they have to deal with failure more than anybody else in the kitchen. They are a special breed of people—maybe from inhaling all of that sugar—but they are looked at with a little suspicion by the rest of the cooks.

In 1993 Ron Siegel made what I consider to be a great culinary contribution to Maine by opening When Pigs Fly, one of the first, if not *the* first, real bread bakery in the state. Now doing business in their hometown of York, Maine, they bake up to eight thousand loaves per day and have reached over one million New Englanders. Their breads, fifteen varieties, are made from all natural ingredients, often organic, with no added fats, preservatives, or dairy. They have their unbleached flour milled for them and say that their "onions are roasted, potatoes are peeled, and olives pitted on a daily basis." A lot of work and love goes into their bread, and a loaf takes thirty-six hours from start to finish. If you want to try When Pigs Fly bread, you can contact them through their website.

Evalin is now a prominent caterer in Portland and comes to Manhattan regularly to eat and shop, not necessarily in that order. Michael Allen is in Vermont running a gorgeous old inn he bought, the Deerhill Inn in the Green Mountains.

Mark is a wonderful, inventive chef, who, with his partner, Clark Frasier, owns Arrows Restaurant in Ogunquit. An old farmhouse at one time, Arrows is the most fulfilling restaurant experience you'll have in Maine, from the endless cutting gardens, to the acres of fresh lettuces, vegetables, and herbs, which end up on their painstaking and extraordinary menu. Each time I go to Maine, I drive to Ogunquit to spend the evening sitting in Mark and Clark's tavern room enjoying the beauty around me and marveling at all they've accomplished and the chef Mark has become. Tall and as slender now as he was then, the only difference I see in Mark is that his hair has grown slightly gray and there's a little less of it. He still has the same kind, wide blue eyes and sweet, ready smile that he had twenty years ago.

The $95 Raspberry

After three years at the Whistling Oyster, I felt I was ready to move on. When the White Barn Inn called to say they were looking for a chef, I took it as a good omen. One of the things I liked best about working in Kennebunkport was the connection I had to my grandmother and the rest of the family by working in places they had visited decades before. The Whistling Oyster had become a restaurant since its days as one of my grandmother's favorite tea salons and being there, working every day, was like being near her in a way. When I walked into the White Barn Inn, formerly the Forest Hill House, it felt nearly as familiar as home.

They told me they wanted a more sophisticated menu that would impress their tony Boston and New York clientele. They said I had carte blanche to achieve this. Very seldom do people mean it when they offer you that kind of freedom, and such was the case here.

When I walked into the White Barn's kitchen for the first time, I was appalled. I went to the pantry and cleared away case after case of Knorr powdered sauce mixes, hollandaise, Bearnaise—you name it. It was even scarier downstairs where there were towering stacks of number-ten cans filled with generic brands of corn, artichokes, tuna fish, and tomatoes. There was an old, wooden walk-in refrigerator that held the only bit of fresh food in sight: one case of iceberg lettuce, one case of very pale tomatoes, and some onions that were growing greenish blue beards. It was very different from Michael's kitchen, which had been pristine with the freshest ingredients available.

I cleaned out the cans and hid the three well-used microwaves from the kitchen down there. I had to replace that mess with real food, but the problem was they wouldn't let me remove most of the stuff they had on the menu. Everything was named after them, or people who worked there, like Jack's Preference, a canned artichoke heart stuffed with canned crabmeat and covered with packaged béarnaise sauce, then put under the broiler for a few minutes. I couldn't wait to get rid of that, but management refused. They insisted that this was a longtime customer favorite and had to stay on the menu. Their unwillingness to let go of these dishes, combined with the difficulty of getting top-quality purveyors to service us way up north, was going to make this an uphill battle.

For instance, one night when I was still at the Whistling Oyster, we needed raspberries for a dessert for a special party. It doesn't seem like a big deal now, but arranging it required the logistical genius of an army general planning a war campaign. As with anything that wasn't in season, raspberries had to be trucked in from Boston because there were few local purveyors. I got my raspberries, but they cost me $95 for six pints! The truck they arrived in should have had BRINK'S printed on the side.

Despite the stumbling blocks, I got the White Barn its four stars and twelve days later, they fired me. They said I didn't take direction well. I told them, "You didn't hire me to take direction, you hired me to give it!" That's when I knew, as much as I loved living in Maine, I wasn't going to grow there as a chef. I knew I would eventually have to leave.

New York, New York

I returned to the city with a plan, which was to work in one of the best restaurants in Manhattan so that I could continue my training. I consulted *Zagat's*, which was a brand-new restaurant guide at the time, made a list of restaurants, and set about writing to some chefs. In addition, I came down to the city on alternate weekends and pounded the pavement—and pound it I did. I wore out a pair of shoes. At the time, the late 1980s, kitchens were male dominated and none of them were interested in taking a chance on me. Only a few even granted me an interview. I still remember with whom I spoke. Drew Nieporent was very kind and generous but didn't need anyone (his chef at the time was David Bouley). As is his way, Drew gave me some solid advice and names of people to talk to.

The country had recently been hit with a wave of women chefs, led by Alice Waters in northern California, Madeleine Kamman in Cambridge,

Massachusetts, and Anne Rosenzweig in New York. Anne had made a name for herself when she opened her signature restaurant Arcadia and quickly became one of the foremost new American chefs in the country. She built her menu around what she called "inventive cuisine." She took her inspiration from any food that interested her, from French to Moroccan. Anne was one of the chefs I had written to, and she not only hired me as a line cook but also made me her sous chef (second in command) two years later.

You learn in every kitchen, and what I learned in Anne's was how to run a small restaurant. I paid close attention and watched as she bargained over the phone with purveyors one minute and sweet-talked celebrities the next. Anne constantly had her eye on the bottom line, but never at the expense of creativity and food quality. She managed to strike the perfect balance on where to save money and where to spend it. When I opened Pearl, that experience helped me more than anything else.

I applied to Anne originally because there was a rustic quality to her cooking that matched my own philosophy. We both liked the idea of taking classic dishes and making them new or preparing them in a way they hadn't been prepared before. Anne's food was known for its whimsy too, and she would come up with great names for dishes.

One night Julia Child came in to Arcadia for dinner with people on the Board of the American Institute of Food and Wine. Anne was away and I was in charge. I wanted everything to be beyond perfect. I was nervous as I watched her from a safe distance. She was wonderful at ordering and took care of the entire table. They ordered wine continually and it was a jubilant table.

Not only was Julia Child in that night, but the former *New York Times* restaurant reviewer Mimi Sheraton came in unexpectedly and was sitting virtually next to her. At the time she had her own newsletter called *Taste,* and she was still reviewing restaurants. There was a party upstairs, a full restaurant, and the tension in the kitchen was almost unbearable.

But it all melted away when Julia Child came back to the kitchen to tell us how much she enjoyed herself. She spent a long time asking questions about how things were prepared, looking over the kitchen and making us all feel that we were the interesting ones.

After Arcadia, I moved on to become the executive chef at a downtown restaurant, which turned out to be a horrendous experience. I was working for a family who knew more about politics than food and whose matriarch threatened that I would never work in this town again when I disagreed with her. I felt like I was in an old Adolphe Menjou movie: "Kid! You'll never work in this town again!" It was a serious moment but it was all I could do not to laugh. Still, it became the most formative restaurant experience of my life because I vowed I really never would work for anyone else in this town again. That's when I started making plans for Pearl.

THE PERFECT GRILLED FISH

WHOLE FISH: This is really the best way to grill fish because it has the skin on and is therefore not going to stick as easily. It also protects the meat, allowing you to expand your choices. Snapper, trout, sea bass, pompano, and dourade would flake and stick if you tried to grill just the fillet, but they are delicious grilled whole with sliced garlic and a variety of herbs stuffed in the cavity. It's also easier because you can get a fish that will feed four people, and still have room on your grill for whatever else you might want to cook.

FISH STEAK: The term can be confusing because there are fish that chefs call steak fish and then there are fish steaks. A fish steak is the cross-section cut you often see with the bone down the center and the skin on. In your fish market, most common examples are salmon, halibut, and Chilean sea bass, which grill well because the skin and bone hold them together.

LOIN: You see sections from the loin cut all the time in a sushi bar. It's the triangular-shaped log of tuna that the chef pulls out to cut the sushi from. For grilling, you would slice these into small steaks, about 1 to $1\frac{1}{2}$ inches thick. The cut grills well because of the texture of this kind of fish, which doesn't flake or come apart naturally.

FILLET AND FLATFISH: Only a fillet fish higher in oil content, like salmon, is good for grilling. Snapper, bass, and trout will all flake apart and are better left whole. Flatfish like flounder, fluke, or sole don't lend themselves to the grill, except for a halibut fillet, which is fairly large.

Grilling Tips

MARINATING: Fish should not be marinated for a long time, especially not in anything acidic, like citrus, wine, or vinegar. That would be ceviche—delicious, but not the dish you're aiming for. When I prepare fish, I marinate it very quickly and simply. I place the fish in a shallow pan, drizzle a little olive oil over the fish, and press fresh herbs into the top. I cover it with plastic wrap for about half an hour. You don't need to leave it any longer than that. I season the fish with salt and pepper just before I grill it.

By simply pairing fish with various herbs you can achieve many different flavors without doing anything substantially different. Being a traditionalist, I particularly like swordfish with dill, salmon with rosemary, tuna with basil, and halibut with marjoram.

Personally, I think that sauces like barbecue, teriyaki, or fruit-based glazes cover up the flavor of the fish. But then I'm a purist. If you do want to use sauces, they need to be put on when the fish is almost cooked, particularly if there is sugar in them. Otherwise the fish will stick to the grill and make a big mess.

PREPARING THE GRILL: Before you start cooking, season the grill with a little oil (any kind). I usually use a couple of saturated rolled-up paper towels. I use regular kitchen utensils, not those two-feet-long tongs and spatulas that come with barbecue sets. They're unwieldy and impossible to use.

Fish grilling requires a very hot fire, built about three to four inches from the grill. You shouldn't be able to hold your hand over the fire for more than two seconds—that's how you know it's hot enough. Make sure that the grill is in place for at least ten minutes before you start, so it's as hot as the fire.

PERFECT GRILL MARKS: The grill is hot, the fish is seasoned, and now it's time to concentrate on grilling. In restaurants, perfect marks are achieved by placing the fish at two o'clock on vertical grill bars and then turning it to four o'clock after the first set of marks are made. You will only be marking one side for presentation. It takes so long to make the marks that you would overcook the fish if you tried it on both sides. If this is too intimidating, one set of marks is fine too. After the second set of marks is made, carefully turn the fish over and continue cooking. For a 1^1/$_2$-inch-thick piece of fish, it will take approximately 4 minutes on the presentation side and 2 minutes after it's turned over. To serve, a final drizzle of extra-virgin olive oil is nice, and plenty of lemon wedges and fresh herbs.

Grilled Halibut with Marjoram

1- or $1^1/4$-inch thick halibut steaks, skin on, one per person

Extra-virgin olive oil

3 to 4 fresh marjoram sprigs

Kosher salt or sea salt and freshly ground black pepper

Lemon wedges

Put the fish steaks in a bowl and drizzle them with the olive oil. Press the sprigs of fresh marjoram into the steaks, cover the bowl, and put in the refrigerator for 1 hour to marinate. Preheat the grill to high heat and set the grill 4 inches from the heat. Remove the marjoram sprigs, season each steak with salt and pepper, and place on the grill. Once the fish is on the grill, *do not move it until it's time to turn it* or the fish will stick and you will not be able to achieve attractive grill marks. Turn the fish only once, and depending on its thickness, cook it on each side for 3 to 4 minutes. When it's done, the fish will be firm to the touch with no trace of translucency. Serve with lemon wedges.

Grilled Whole Fish

1- to $1^1/4$-pound snapper, sea bass, pompano, or dourade,
    one per person

Herbs such as thyme, rosemary, oregano, and marjoram

2 garlic cloves, thinly sliced, per fish

Lemon slices

Olive oil

Kosher salt and freshly ground black pepper

Lemon wedges

Ask your fishmonger for a scaled, cleaned, and gutted fish. Wash the fish thoroughly and pat it dry with paper towels.

Start a fire in your grill. In 30 minutes, when the coals turn white, it will be ready to use. With a sharp knife, score the fish right to the spine with 3 slits on each side a couple of inches apart. Stuff the fish with herbs, sliced garlic, and lemon slices. Rub the fish all over with olive oil and season it liberally with salt and pepper. Rub a little oil on the grill and lay the fish over the hot fire for 4 or 5 minutes. To turn the fish, put the spatula under the mouth of the fish, slide it firmly under it, and flip. Cook on the other side for about 5 minutes. When the fish is done, the flesh in the scored area will have lost its translucency and be firm and white at the bone. Using the spatula under the head of the fish and being careful not to disturb the skin, lift it off the grill and put it on a platter. Garnish it with more herbs and lemon wedges.

Sauces

It's great to have sauces to go with fish in your cooking repertoire. Here is the basic recipe for butter sauce, which is delicious on any fish. But you can flavor the sauce in many different ways to change the dish.

Butter Sauce

$1/4$ cup white wine

$1/4$ cup white wine vinegar

2 chopped shallots

$1/2$ pound unsalted butter, cut into small pieces

Kosher salt and freshly ground black pepper

In a stainless steel saucepan over medium heat, combine the white wine, vinegar, and shallots. Bring to a simmer and reduce until you have about 1 tablespoon of the liquid left. Temperature control is very important, because butter sauces break; reduce the heat to low and add the butter one piece at a time. As the butter starts to melt and the sauce catches, you can add the butter more quickly and raise the temperature slightly. Whisk it constantly. As soon as you see that all the butter has melted, turn off the heat; too much heat at this point will break the sauce. Season to taste with salt and pepper. Keep in a warm place until ready to use.

Butter Sauce Variations

cooked puréed corn or chopped tarragon	grilled lobster
chopped tomato and chive	pan-roasted scallops
grated horseradish and mustard	salmon
lemon and caper	any kind of fish, especially sole, skate, haddock, and cod
chopped thyme, tarragon, or chervil	any fish

Basil Oil

Basil oil, any kind of herb oil actually, can be drizzled over fish after you've cooked it and is especially good on grilled fish.

2 cups fresh basil leaves, washed
2 cups extra-virgin olive oil

Blanch the basil leaves and shock in cold water. Drain and squeeze dry, then purée with a couple of tablespoons of oil in a blender. Add the rest of the oil in a steady stream. It keeps for about 1 week refrigerated.

Pearle and Pearl

BY 1993 I HAD SPENT MORE THAN FIFTEEN YEARS COOKING IN OTHER PEOPLE'S RESTAURANTS IN BOTH NEW YORK CITY AND MAINE. Disenchanted would be the nice word to use for how I was feeling, and I was determined to open my own place. Of course, as anyone who has ever opened a restaurant will tell you, determination is not everything.

I use this photo of my grandmother on business cards for Pearl, my restaurant.

Money helps a lot, and a lot of money helps even more. By watching what I spent (I can make a chicken last longer than anyone you know) and renting the living room of a friend's one-bedroom apartment long after a grown-up should stop having a roommate, I had saved over $75,000 of my own money for the project. It was necessary and I knew it because I had learned my lesson about *investors* when I was working as a chef in Kennebunkport.

Somewhere around 1985 or 1986, after some solid experience and decent reviews, I thought I was ready to open my own restaurant in Kennebunkport. There were plenty of culinary voids in Maine to fill at that time, but I had my heart set on the classic French bistro serving some of my own favorite foods like beef marrow, brandade, confit, and cassoulet. Since the restaurants I had worked in were well-known in the area, I had fed quite a few well-heeled people. In the soft afterglow of being well fed, they threw all sorts of investment money at my clogs—metaphorically, anyway.

When the last restaurant I worked in closed, I began calling my metaphoric investors who wished me well but seemed to forget the promises made over plates of pan-roasted quail with potato and shallot tumbleweed and pickled red cabbage. There went my first restaurant.

In Maine I had begun looking at potential restaurant sites, and I found that I really loved this part of the process. Later, when I was trying to open Pearl, it was the same fascination. Talking to agents, comparing spaces, learning how to make an offer—I was learning something every day. They were also invaluable in understanding the myriad neighborhoods within a neighborhood that make up Manhattan. To this day I enjoy matching up chef friends who want to open their own restaurants with spaces that I come across as I continue to follow the changing landscape of real estate in New York.

But while the looking and learning is fun, the finding can be a nightmare. As horrific as it can be to find your dream house or, worse yet, a habitable New York City apartment, it is nothing compared to the challenge of actually finding a restaurant space—especially in Manhattan. To make it even more difficult, I chose Greenwich Village, where there is a paucity of space to begin with. Each time I found a potential home for Pearl, I would spend weeks on the market research for that particular neighborhood and then write a detailed business plan. I must have put together fifteen complete business plans over two years, including the final one for Pearl Oyster Bar. But that plan actually secured a loan for me. As I said, the new skills you pick up while working on a project like this are surprising. The Small Business Administration put my business plan in their textbook as an example for others wanting to open a business. When people come to eat because they've seen the plan in a business school book, it is satisfying to know that all of the work I did helped more than just me.

Originally, Pearl was supposed to be a fifty-five seat, white tablecloth dining experience that served regional American food. But the reality of finding decent real estate was a challenge. For three years, I would continually close in on a space, business plan researched and written, only to have something go wrong. Sometimes the owner or landlord wanted too much money. Other times he did not think I was a good risk because I was a first-time business owner, generally referred to as a start-up. There were numerous times when the lease would go to someone with an existing restaurant or business and a track record. By September 1996, I had spent three years employed only at the business of opening my restaurant. I was frustrated and ready to give up my dream. I was exhausted, there didn't seem to be any spaces on the horizon, and my savings had dwindled to around $50,000—even I can stretch chicken only so far. That meant I was now forced to abandon the more elegant white-tablecloth restaurant I had been planning and find a smaller concept that could be mounted with my ever shrinking finances, or I could leave the city altogether and go back to Maine where my money would go further and landlords were more flexible.

Although it was going to cut into my savings, I needed a vacation. At the time, it seemed considerably cheaper than six months at a private mental health clinic later on. For years I had wanted to visit Napa Valley's wineries and San Francisco, which had become a restaurant town. When I got off the plane in California, I headed straight to the Swan Oyster Depot, which I had been reading about in a guidebook. For anyone who has spent time in Maine, steamers, oysters, and beer are comfort food, and it was the perfect way to relax on my first real vacation in at least five years. But just moments after ordering an icy pint of pilsner, it became a working vacation. Sitting on one of the stools of the famous old oyster bar, a fixture for seafood aficionados, including legendary food writer M. F. K. Fisher, a lightbulb appeared over my head like in a cartoon. I realized what I could do with the money I had left.

Swan's tiny fifteen-seat counter in a closetlike space gave me hope. There was minimal, if any, cooking going on. I liked the layout—the open kitchen and the way the guys behind the counter did everything from cracking the great, prehistoric-looking Dungeness crabs and shucking the briny, glistening

West Coast oysters to pouring beer and wine and serving the customers. There were no tables. I might not have been able to afford white tablecloths, but I could still afford stools. Unlike Swan's San Francisco–style seafood, I would draw on my long family history with New England seafood—Maine specifically—to create Pearl's menu. In a couple of hours I had worked the entire menu out in my head.

Cornelia Street

The little counter at Pearl.

Within a few weeks after returning home to New York, I had found the perfect little space on Cornelia Street in Greenwich Village—a street I had been coveting for years.

When I called to take the space at 18 Cornelia Street, I got devastating news. It had been rented before I even looked at it. To say I was heartbroken would be an understatement. The man who had shown me the space reminded me that leases fell through all the time and told me to call back periodically to check. The problem was that I had my heart set on this space. I called every week until it was just a task, and I didn't really expect good news. But on one of my calls in late October, I was told the deal fell through. "Get the lease ready," I said. "I'll be right over." Within an hour I had that lease in my hand. With several restaurants already on the short block, the street was quickly garnering a reputation as the new restaurant row.

I was back to needing money and after my experience in Maine with investors, I approached the Small Business Development Center at Pace University. They had been advising me for years about a loan, and did help me secure one from the SBA's inaugural Women's Prequalification Program for $60,000. This was in addition to the more than $40,000 I invested and the $15,000 from my mother and our family friend Redmond J. McConnell. I invited a former Cascabel line cook to be a junior partner and Pearl's sous chef, and she put in $8,000. All together it allowed me to open the door of Pearl for just over $120,000.

Although the space was a mess, it was the right size and the right price, and had very popular restaurants nearby. Barbara Shinn and David Page had been the Cornelia Street pioneers in 1993 with their restaurant Home, one door down from Pearl. Mario Batali, who had just gotten his own TV show on the Food Network, was right across the street in his first restaurant, Po. The Cornelia Street Café was across the street from me too; they had opened their doors back in 1976 with a hot plate and an espresso machine. I could not have devised a better marketing plan, but what I did not know and could not have predicted was the support and friendship I got from these chefs. We share bread and blowtorches, linens and butter—whatever we have that the other needs. In the beginning, David was invaluable at alerting me to certain food critics lurking clandestinely at my bar. Mario was quick with all kinds of advice and spent many evenings seeking refuge from his bustling restaurant and burgeoning fame, sitting on a milk crate in my backyard while I fed him fried oysters, steamers, and beer.

Restaurant Leslie

Cornelia Street also brought back great food memories from my earliest years cooking in the city. When I was just starting out as a line cook in the late 1970s, my favorite place to eat had been on the street. Restaurant Leslie, opened by chef Leslie Revsin, considered by many to be the first high-profile woman chef and restaurant owner in the city, had been where Home now was, or so I thought. I had had many incredible meals at Restaurant Leslie including many firsts—my first sweetbreads, as prepared by Leslie, were tender and crispy sweet, and difficult for others to live up to in the future. She also had French specialties that I had never had the opportunity to eat before, like quenelles and these truly remarkable Roquefort beignets, a light, buttery cloud filled with a molten center of the rich French cheese. They almost brought tears to your eyes, they were so good. As always with me, my *favorite* dish was fairly simple: a double breast of chicken with a rich mustard crust that was absolutely delicious—to this day I cannot figure out how she made it.

But it wasn't the particular dishes that made the restaurant so special, it was the cooking, the one thing people underestimate all the time. I do not care if all you are making is a grilled cheese sandwich as long as you prepare it as perfectly as possible and it tastes great. Tom Colicchio, the executive chef of Danny Meyer's Gramercy Tavern and owner of Craft, is a master at what I call the art of preparing simple food well. Spare me architecturally unbalanced food with too many flavors that fight each other for prominence. Fusion? To me it's confusion. When I walk into Craft I know that my sirloin will be the best meat available, seasoned and cooked perfectly, and I know it will taste exactly as I hoped it would. That is what I strive for every day as a chef.

One night I had a particularly special meal at Restaurant Leslie, although that night it had little to do with what we ate. A friend who had been a partner in the business called to tell me that one of my heroines, Lillian Hellman, had a reservation that evening to have dinner with screen legend Claudette Colbert. For a onetime aspiring playwright and film director, the combination was heady. Since I was very young, the only person I could think of who would appreciate this as much as me was my mom. So I made her come in from New Rochelle and hours later we were having our dinner elbow to elbow with them. I cannot tell you much about it because I was studiously trying to look nonchalant and because they were sitting so close that the slightest glimpse would have been obvious. But they spoke in hushed voices, chain-smoked incessantly, and indulged in a seemingly never-ending stream of cocktails. I felt like I was holding my breath the whole time.

Twenty years later, while Pearl was under construction, I was speaking to David Page about Restaurant Leslie, and he said his space had been a Cuban place but didn't know what mine had been. The place had been such a disaster when I took it over that it never occurred to me it might have been Restaurant Leslie. But a few days later as the workmen were removing the old front door, which had wasted away and was hollow, there was a huge wad of old mail, most of it addressed to Restaurant Leslie!

The Cod That Made Me Cry

Pearl Oyster Bar was just an idea, inspired by the many lobster shacks that have passed through my life, and one of the best things about opening Pearl was finally making the lobster roll what I knew it could be. What I never could have foreseen was the way Manhattan would take to the sandwich.

When I was a child, my Kennebunkport summers were synonymous with two food items: lobster rolls and blueberry pie. Fond, almost romantic, memories of these beach classics followed me for more than forty years. But as I grew older, I realized that the lobster roll often didn't live up to my ideal. Frankly, even some of the most famous lobster rolls aren't particularly good ones. But that's because, as with all simple food, a lot can go wrong when you're making a lobster roll.

For instance, cooking lobster and then picking it is labor intensive, so many places buy the lobster meat already packaged or—and this is an abomination—frozen. Even if they do use fresh lobster, it can often be overcooked, affecting the texture of the salad. Then there are other variables, from type of mayonnaise and bun, to whether or not the bun is toasted and whether it is toasted with or without butter, to what else someone might be tempted to throw into the mix in the misguided name of being creative.

When I decided to put the humble Maine staple on Pearl's menu, I never expected to start a revolution. After all, clam shacks had been putting lobster rolls on their menus for more than fifty years. No one remembers exactly who invented the sandwich, although no shortage of New England teashops, clam shacks, and lobster pounds are probably willing to take the credit. My guess is that it was some old Maine lobsterman's wife relentlessly long on lobster but short on ideas who, faced with a refrigerator filled with cooked lobster, decided to give it the tuna salad treatment. In food, excess is often the mother of invention.

I like to think that the difference in our lobster roll is that at Pearl we emphasize the importance of cooking technique, thereby elevating the simple recipes and the food itself. I have customers who have been coming to Pearl for years and simply cannot order anything else, try as they might. They sit there and look at the menu; I can see it in their eyes—they want to try something different, want to order seared scallops or bouillabaisse, or venture out into the world of the whole grilled fish. But pretty soon they look up, guilt shimmering in their eyes, and order the lobster roll. It is amazing the number of New York City menus that feature the lobster roll now. And it is very satisfying—in fact it pleases me to no end—that the Maine lobster roll is fast becoming a New York sandwich.

All I ever wanted to do was open a little restaurant. It's why I still work the line. There are mornings that I go into Pearl and am perfectly happy to be up to my elbows filleting fish. Pompano happens to be the cutest fish in the world, docile with sweet eyes and tiny smiles on their butter-yellow faces. Recently I had a plump, fresh cod come in that was so beautiful—the snowy white firmness of the flesh—that it nearly made me cry.

The best part of Pearl is that it becomes its own world, a working piece of the neighborhood, and yet set apart from it in some way. Many of our customers are like family, and if they don't come in for awhile, we wonder and worry. They have nicknames like a Dick Tracy cartoon. Toga Lady—elegant, regal, and always in long, swooping clothes that you might see on a dancer—

reapplies her lipstick after every meal with grace and swiftness we watch and admire. The Grumpies have been coming in forever, and we think come mostly to complain and torture us about dishes we take off the menu. I have gone to memorial services for dear friends, such as one of Pearl's most ardent supporters, the wonderful Alice Trillin, food lover and wife of Bud Trillin. There have been babies to buy gifts for and weddings to toast with champagne.

There are nights when the restaurant moves like a samba, in perfect time. Everyone is having fun, strangers have struck up conversations, and seats empty and refill without the evening skipping a beat. As a chef who gets to be within earshot of the customers, most nights it allows for a lively conversation about food rolling up and down the bar. Someone will tell you what dish they love at an old place or what to avoid at a new spot. Everyone weighs in, and I learn more about what's going on in the restaurant business than I have since Gael Greene stopped writing the weekly restaurant review for *New York* magazine.

This is what I have always wanted, and every time I think about venturing out into another restaurant, I get a little pang. Without even leaving, I am anticipating being homesick for my little restaurant.

PEARL CLASSICS

Small Plates

Gazpacho with Lobster and Shrimp
Serves 4

Don't be confined to using these colors or varieties of tomatoes. Heirloom tomatoes in summer, for instance, would be a nice addition.

1 large garlic clove
Kosher salt and freshly ground black pepper
2 medium red bell peppers, cut into small dice
2 medium cucumbers, seeded, peeled, and cut into small dice (or 4 to 5 Kirbys with seeds)
5 medium vine-ripened tomatoes, cut into small dice
1 medium jalapeño pepper, seeded and minced (optional)
1 quart tomato juice
1 lemon, juiced
2 cooked chilled lobster tails
8 cooked chilled shrimp
Chopped chives

On a cutting board, smash the garlic clove with the back of your knife, cover it with salt, and let it sit for 5 minutes. Then work it into a paste with the back of your knife and finish by chopping it. It will seem almost puréed at that point. Combine the rest of the ingredients (except the lobster, shrimp, and chives) in a large bowl and stir thoroughly. Season to taste. The gazpacho should sit for 2 hours before serving and will keep, covered, for 3 or 4 days in the refrigerator.

To serve, slice the lobster into $1/4$-inch medallions. Slice the shrimp in half lengthwise. Ladle the soup into the bowls, garnish with the sliced shellfish, and sprinkle with the chives.

Salt-Crusted Shrimp

Serves 4, as an appetizer

When I worked at Arcadia, Anne Rosenzweig would occasionally take her cooks down to Chinatown to eat. One of the dishes she almost always ordered was salt and pepper shrimp. I didn't know that anything could be eaten shell and all except for soft-shell crabs. The restaurant, which I think was called the Phoenix Garden, was very near the amusement arcade that featured a counting chicken. Pearl regular and author/food authority Calvin Trillin was fond of writing about the chicken and made her famous. I used to pass her with my friend Tony Bonner, a line cook at Arcadia, when we went down there after work to eat.

Salt-crusted shrimp has become a favorite of mine. It's always exciting the first time you eat anything fried with the shell on, whether it's soft-shell crabs or shrimp. There is an exhilarating kind of fear. I love the delicate rice-paper-thin crispness of the shell, coated generously with cracked black pepper and salt. When you bite down you get that first crunchy snap, and then you taste the shrimp, piping hot and juicy. The nice thing about shrimp fried this way is the absence of the heavy flour or batter coating—you actually taste the shrimp better. The Chinese way of preparing this dish is to bake it, but Pearl's salt-crusted shrimp is deep-fried to make it even crispier.

At the restaurant we serve this with a little cold vegetable salad, tossed with a light vinaigrette, and tartar sauce. Sometimes we serve a cucumber, tomato, and red onion with dill salad, and other times a salad of haricots verts, red pepper, and celery with tarragon. But you can make a little salad out of anything.

Vegetable, peanut, or canola oil

1 cup flour

$^1/_3$ cup cracker meal

12 medium shrimp, deveined, shell on

Kosher salt and freshly ground black pepper

In a 5-quart saucepot heat 4 cups of oil to 350°F. In a pie plate, combine the flour and cracker meal. Dredge the shrimp thoroughly in the flour mixture. Shake off the excess. If you don't have a thermometer, drop a test shrimp into the oil. If it sizzles and rises to the surface immediately, it's ready. Fry the shrimp for about 2 minutes, then drain on paper towels. Season aggressively with salt and pepper on both sides.

Johnnycakes with Smoked Salmon and Crème Fraîche

Serves 4 to 6 as an appetizer

If not for Native Americans and their way with corn, it is doubtful that the European settlements would have taken hold when they did. Native Americans had been roasting corn and grinding it into meal for centuries before settlers arrived. They baked it into cakes and mush, breads and porridges, and although these foods were instrumental in the survival of the settlers, they looked down upon them as years went by. The transplanted English were used to wheat flour as well as cooking with iron pans, not layering wet corn dough onto ash-covered stone or the blades of upright hoes, as the Indians did. Johnnycake and corn bread seem to have started out as the same thing, with names that included corn pone, journey cakes, ashcakes, spoonbread, and hoe-cakes. At some point, johnnycakes were to the North what corn bread was to the South, although even within an area like New England the meanings could sway. Johnnycake in Maine, Vermont, New Hampshire, and parts of Massachusetts was leavened bread, whereas in Rhode Island, it was a thinner batter made into a pancake. The latter is what I make, but what all these batters have in common is that they are made of corn.

For the Batter

1 egg
1 cup good-quality cornmeal
1¾ cups milk
½ cup butter, melted
Pinch of kosher salt

18 slices smoked salmon
6 teaspoons crème fraîche (sour cream can be substituted)
2 tablespoons thinly sliced chives
Flat-leaf parsley leaves for garnish

In a large bowl, combine the egg, cornmeal, milk, ¼ cup of the melted butter, and salt and whisk thoroughly. Let stand for 30 minutes. Heat a 6-inch nonstick skillet over medium heat. Using a paper towel, wipe the inside of the pan with a generous amount of the remaining melted butter. Pour ¼ cup of batter into the pan. When the top of the pancake looks set and the tiny bubbles have burst, it's time to flip it. Use a plastic spatula to loosen the edges, shake it a couple of times, and flip. If you are scared to do this, use your spatula to turn it over. Fifteen seconds on the other side should finish the pancake. Stack them on a plate covered with a clean kitchen towel while you make the other pancakes.

Center each pancake on a dinner plate and drape 3 slices of smoked salmon in the middle of each. Top with a teaspoon of crème fraîche and sprinkle the entire dish sparingly with chives. Stand a leaf of parsley in the dollop of crème fraîche and serve.

Pearl Oyster Bar Crabcakes

Serves 4

1 teaspoon Dijon mustard

1 teaspoon Colman's dry mustard

2 shakes of Tabasco sauce (or your favorite hot sauce)

4 shakes of Worcestershire sauce

Kosher salt and freshly ground black pepper

2 eggs

Juice of $1/4$ lemon

1 teaspoon chopped chives

1 pound jumbo lump crabmeat, picked through to remove any shells

1 tablespoon diced and seeded tomato

$1/2$ cup toasted bread crumbs (homemade is best, but packaged is fine)

$1/2$ cup clarified butter (page 62)

4 to 6 lemon wedges

Italian parsley leaves for garnish

Chopped chives for garnish

In a large bowl, whisk to combine the mustards, Tabasco, Worcestershire, pinch of salt and pepper, the eggs, and lemon juice.

Add the teaspoon of chives, crabmeat, tomato, and bread crumbs and toss gently by hand.

To assemble the crabcakes, press the mixture into a $1/2$-cup measuring cup to form it. Unmold it on bread crumbs that are spread out on a sheet pan. Refrigerate it on the pan for about 30 minutes, or until it's set. Remove the crabcakes from the refrigerator. Picking up the crabcakes one at a time, sprinkle the bread crumbs liberally over both sides. Press them well with both hands and let the excess fall off. Place the finished crabcakes in a container until you are ready to sauté them. These can be made up to a day in advance. If using immediately, refrigerate for about 30 minutes, covered.

Preheat the oven to 450°F. In a large ovenproof sauté pan over medium heat, sauté the crabcakes in clarified butter on one side until golden brown. Flip them and finish the crabcakes in the oven for 3 to 4 minutes, or until golden brown.

Serve the crabcakes with lemon wedges and sprinkle them with Italian parsley leaves and chopped chives. To make a lunch out of the crabcakes, the slaws (pages 66–67) and Sweet Corn Ragout (page 69) are perfect accompaniments.

Large Plates

Pearl Oyster Bar Lobster Roll

Serves 2

You can get lobster rolls anywhere in Maine, even at McDonald's. There are two traditional ways to prepare them, the first being a warm sandwich with lobster chunks sautéed in butter and piled into the bun. This to me usually just winds up being overly greasy—why not have hot boiled lobster with drawn butter instead? My favorite is the mayonnaisey lobster salad in a butter-toasted bun.

It is best to cook your own lobsters at home and pick the meat. Precooked meat is generally overcooked, probably not fresh, and definitely overpriced.

There are two kinds of hot dog buns. I classify them like washing machines, top loaders and side loaders. The quintessential Maine lobster roll is made with a top-loading bun, which has a flat side that keeps everything from flopping over and spilling out. New York City, on the other hand, is a side loading town, so I have mine special delivered by Pepperidge Farm.

At Pearl Oyster Bar, we serve the lobster roll in a way that Mainers would consider pretty upscale. We fill the bun with the lobster salad, sprinkle it with chopped chives, and put it next to a big pile of shoestring fries, with a garnish of baby greens. The traditional garnish is a couple of slices of bread and butter pickles and a big mound of potato chips.

2 pounds cooked lobster meat, chopped roughly into $1/2$- and $3/4$-inch pieces

$1/2$ celery rib, finely chopped

$1/4$ cup Hellmann's mayonnaise

Squeeze of lemon

Pinch of kosher salt and freshly ground black pepper

2 teaspoons unsalted butter

2 Pepperidge Farm top-loading hot dog buns

Chopped chives for garnish

To make the lobster salad, in a large bowl, combine the lobster meat, celery, mayonnaise, lemon, and salt and pepper and mix thoroughly. Cover the mixture and store it in the refrigerator until ready to serve. It will last for up to 2 days.

To prepare the bun, in a small sauté pan over low to medium heat, melt the butter. Place the hot dog buns on their sides in the butter. Flip the buns a couple of times so that both sides soak up an equal amount of butter and brown evenly. Remove the buns from the pan and place them on a large plate.

Fill the toasted buns with the lobster salad. Sprinkle with chives and serve with a salad, slaw, or shoestring fries.

Variation: For a shrimp roll, substitute 2 pounds of shrimp, cooked, peeled, and sliced in half lengthwise.

Pearl Oyster Bar Oyster Roll

Serves 2

New Englanders will stuff just about anything into a hot dog bun. Of course, the hot dog roll must be a top loader and is best when sautéed in butter until each side is golden. Then you can fill it with shrimp, tuna, or lobster salad, fried clams, scallops, or lobster meat and you have a classic New England roll. At Pearl Oyster Bar, we like to fill the rolls up with tartar sauce and plump fried oysters, so hot that their juices squirt out when you bite into them. As popular as the Pearl Lobster Roll is for us, there are devotees of the oyster roll who wouldn't think of ordering anything else from our lunch menu.

Fried Oysters (page 157)
2 teaspoons unsalted butter
2 Pepperidge Farm top-loading hot dog buns
Pearl Oyster Bar Tartar Sauce (page 157)

To prepare the oysters, fry them as directed.

Prepare the bun as you would for the lobster roll (page 210).

Spread the tartar sauce in the bottom of each bun. Place the fried oysters on the tartar sauce and serve with shoestring fries.

Mussels with White Wine, Shallots, and Mustard

Serves 2

This dish is great served with a crusty baguette to sop up the sauce.

$^1/_3$ cup white wine

2 shallots, finely chopped

2 pounds (30 to 40) cultivated mussels, cleaned and debearded

$^3/_4$ cup heavy cream

1 heaping teaspoon Dijon mustard

Pinch of freshly ground black pepper

Flat-leaf parsley sprigs for garnish

Chopped chives for garnish

In a 10-inch saucepan or pot over high heat, bring the wine, lobster stock, shallots, leek, and fennel to a simmer. Add the mussels and cover the pan. The mussels will open in 3 to 4 minutes. Shaking the pan a couple of times will help the process. Remove the mussels from the pan and place them in a large serving bowl or individual serving bowls. Cover with a towel to keep them warm while you finish the sauce.

To finish the sauce, on high heat, add the heavy cream, mustard, and pepper. Whisk until smooth and reduce until the sauce is slightly thickened and coats the back of a spoon, about 3 or 4 minutes. Pour the sauce over the mussels and garnish with parsley sprigs and chives.

Mussels with Leeks, Fennel, and Tomatoes in Broth

Serves 2

$1/3$ cup white wine

1 cup Lobster Stock (page 174)

2 shallots, finely chopped

1 small leek, cut in half lengthwise, washed, and cut into $1/8$-inch slices

$1/4$ fennel bulb, thinly sliced

2 pounds (30 to 40) cultivated mussels, cleaned, beards removed

$1/2$ vine-ripened tomato, seeded and chopped

Freshly ground black pepper

Kosher salt

Butter (optional)

Chopped chives

Flat-leaf parsley for garnish

In a 10-inch saucepan or pot over high heat, bring the wine, lobster stock, shallots, leek, and fennel to a simmer. Add the mussels and cover the pan. The mussels will open in 3 to 4 minutes; shaking the pan a couple of times will help the process. Remove the mussels from the pan and place them in a large serving bowl or individual serving bowls. Cover with a towel to keep them warm while you finish the sauce.

To finish the sauce, add the chopped tomato to the broth and a couple of grinds of black pepper. Add salt to taste. At this point, you can enrich the sauce with a nub of butter if you like. Add the chives to the sauce before serving and pour over the mussels. Garnish with the parsley leaves.

Soft-shell Crabs

Serves 4

Soft-shell crabs come in three sizes: jumbo, prime, and hotels. There's no better or worse, just bigger and smaller. If you're serving jumbos, one per person will do. If you are using primes, you'll need two, and if you can get only hotels, you'll be using three.

4 jumbo soft-shell crabs
2 cups milk
Kosher salt and freshly ground black pepper
1 cup flour
$1/3$ cup cracker meal
2 cups peanut, canola, or vegetable oil

Use sharp scissors to cut a strip off the top of the crabs, removing the eyes. Lift the left and right sides of the top, and with your fingers, pull out the lungs. Pour the milk into a large bowl. Soak the crabs in the milk for 5 to 10 minutes and drain in a strainer. Place the crabs on a platter and lightly season with salt and pepper. In a pie plate, make a dredge of the flour and cracker meal. Dredge the crabs in the mixture and pat off the excess.

In a large frying pan, heat the oil over medium heat and place the crabs, belly-side down, in the hot oil. (Place the pan on the back burner because soft-shell crabs contain a lot of water and can spit ferociously.) Cook the crabs to a golden brown, or for about 3 minutes. Using tongs, turn them and cook for 1 or 2 minutes more, or until golden brown. Remove the crabs from the pan and drain on paper towels. Serve with the Sweet Corn Ragout (page 69) or Sugar Snap Peas with Lemon and Toasted Almonds (page 63).

Bouillabaisse

Serves 2

The traditional garnish for this dish is a crouton topped with aioli.

2 3-ounce fish fillets (cod, bass, grouper, or snapper)
Kosher salt and freshly ground black pepper
1/4 cup flour
1 1-pound live lobster
2 tablespoons olive oil
2 large sea scallops, muscles removed
2 medium shrimp, shelled and deveined
4 littleneck clams
10 mussels
2 cups Lobster Stock (page 174)
1 teaspoon unsalted butter
Chopped chives for garnish
Flat-leaf parsley for garnish

For the aioli crouton

1 garlic clove
2 egg yolks
2 or 3 saffron threads
Juice of 1/2 lemon
1 cup olive oil for cooking
Kosher salt and freshly ground black pepper
1 baguette or ficelle

Season the fish fillets lightly with salt and pepper. Dredge the fish fillets in flour and pat off the excess. Set aside.

Cut the lobster in half lengthwise. Pull off the claws with knuckles attached. Crack the claws. With a knife, cut off the tail pieces. Put the body in the freezer for stock.

In a 10-inch saucepan, over medium-high heat, add the olive oil. Sauté the scallops, lobster tails and claws, and fish fillets for 2 minutes, until the fillets and scallops are golden brown on one side. Turn them over and add the shrimp and clams. Sauté the shrimp for a minute until they're pink. Add the mussels and the lobster stock. Cover the pan and cook until the mussels open, 3 to 4 minutes. Reduce the heat to low and, using a slotted spoon or tongs, remove all the fish and pile it up in the center of two large, shallow bowls.

Add the butter and season the broth to taste with salt and pepper. Add the chopped chives and pour the broth into the bowls.

To make the aioli, in a food processor, combine the garlic, egg yolks, saffron, and lemon juice. In a slow, steady stream, add $1/2$ cup olive oil while pulsing the machine. Adjust with a few drops of water if it is too thick. Season with salt and pepper. To make the croutons, cut a baguette or ficelle on the bias into 3-inch-long pieces that are about $1/2$ inch wide. In a small sauté pan over medium heat, heat the remaining $1/2$ cup olive oil and fry the bread slices until they are brown on both sides, about 4 minutes. Drain the croutons on paper towels, rub on both sides with a garlic clove, and salt lightly.

To serve, put a teaspoonful of aioli on the crouton. Sprinkle the broth with parsley leaves for garnish and lean the aioli crouton up against the fish.

Aioli Tip

In the spring and summer, when garlic is new, you can use raw cloves. In the fall and winter, when garlic is sprouting and can be very sharp, I use a combination of raw and roasted, which gives the aioli a mellower flavor.

To roast the garlic, preheat the oven to 300°F. Cut a garlic bulb in half at the equator, drizzle with olive oil, and sprinkle with a little salt. Wrap with aluminum foil and bake until it caramelizes, about 45 to 50 minutes.

Back to Gooch's Beach

OWNING A RESTAURANT IN MANHATTAN HAS DEFINITELY CUT DOWN ON THE TIME I CAN SPEND IN MAINE. We go up every Memorial Day to start the summer, on the Fourth of July when we can find a room for a few nights, and always for a few weeks at the end of August during the restaurant's summer vacation. Before I can go anywhere, though, there are myriad things that need to be done to Pearl first. It's amazing the beating that little place takes during the year.

The boys from the kitchen and I take buckets of hot, soapy water and scrub down the kitchen, which has turned brown and sticky from cooking fumes. Then I rummage around through old paint cans in the basement searching for the original paint samples so I can figure out what colors I used. Usually it takes a coat of primer and one coat of paint before the kitchen even starts to come back to life. I paint the outside and every other year I paint the dining room. The maple wood floor is so badly scuffed and marred that it looks black by the end of July, so it needs to be sanded and refinished. All of the cooking equipment and refrigerators get a late summer cleaning, and all of the bills are paid and correspondences answered. Then, and only then, can I relax and enjoy my vacation in Kennebunkport.

On the beach house porch, 1968, David, Pearle, me, and my mom.

Shortly after I came back to Manhattan to live, my mother decided to start renting out our house. My mother was working long hours for the *New*

York Times, which was consuming, and once I became a sous chef in the city, I almost never had time off. Additionally, enormous historic houses have enormous maintenance bills and property taxes.

Being relegated to tourist status once again meant that we had to find a place to stay. Although the Forest Hill House still existed in the form of the elegant White Barn Inn, it is an expensive *uber*-inn that would break the average person who wanted to spend an entire week or more. (If Mrs. Toothaker and Pearle knew how far the hotel had wandered from its simple roots or how much it cost to rent a suite for the night, they would be rolling in their respective graves.)

There are so many wonderful places to stay in the Kennebunks but without knowing it, I think I was really searching for something that reminded me of my grandmother and the family vacations at the shore, which still held some mysterious quality for me. The place that finally made me comfortable was the Seaside Motor Lodge, which wouldn't remind anyone of the Forest Hill House, although it is almost right across the street. But after staying there a few times, I realized that what my grandmother found at the Forest Hill House nearly a century ago I find today at the Seaside.

Originally called the Seaside House, it is the oldest inn in New England, though the Gooch family descendants are forbidden from making that claim. They closed down their inn for a few years when they were run off their land by Indians and had to hole up, what was left of them, in a nearby fort. Since they could not operate continuously during the last 360-plus years, various historical societies have refused to give them the title. The twelfth generation of Gooch descendants have been running the Seaside since the summer of 2001 when Trish and Ken Mason took it over from Trish's dad and mom, Mike and Sandy Severance. Although, in truth, we all suspect it's really the thirteenth generation, Trish and Ken's three-year-old son Jack, who runs the place. He's not in kindergarten yet, but even he can tell you that the exquisite stretch of beach his eleventh great-grandfather, John Gooch the Elder, managed to acquire is better than any old title.

The Promiscuous Preacher

Who knew that a promiscuous preacher from the 1600s would be indirectly responsible for some of my most pleasant vacations? John Gooch the Elder came to innkeeping by accident. He and his wife, Ruth, had come from Slimburg in the United Kingdom to settle in the New World, and ended up in Wells, Maine. Sandy Severance has told me the story of the Seaside, as has her daughter Trish. Both stories match perfectly except for one small detail that Sandy, who is protective of her husband's family history, left out. According to Trish, one of the local preachers coveted not only his neighbor's wife but most of the ladies in the congregation, and he used the power of his pulpit to lure them into illicit romance. Whether Ruth actually transgressed with the preacher or John was just concerned that she was next in the liturgy, so to speak, is unclear, but he decided to move.

At that time, the middle 1600s, England was giving away parcels of land to settlers willing to perform services they deemed necessary. In 1640, King Charles I wanted a ferry to run back and forth across the Kennebunk River. Somehow John Gooch the Elder learned about this. He decided to accept the job as ferryman in the Kennebunks, along with the several acres of oceanfront property that came with it, allowing him to move his pretty young wife out of the preacher's grasp. (The preacher did not fare as well and was eventually tarred and feathered for his sins by the good citizens of Wells.)

Then in 1667, Gooch built an inn to service traders and visitors coming in on the great English ships. The descendants of John the Elder and Younger did well, but for the next two hundred years the struggle to survive was a conquest over nature. Winters were hard and crops were still not growing regularly, though they would eventually have extensive orchards and profuse vegetable gardens. In the summer lobsters washed up on shore and they often collected them for dinner (even though they were used then mostly as fertilizer).

Gooch the Elder built a two-story homestead where he would raise his family, as would John Gooch the Younger, to whom he left the Seaside, and Benjamin Gooch after him. Sadly, though, the Gooch homestead, which also

The Gooches. Right to left: Elizabeth Boothby Gooch (seventh generation), Papa Joe (eighth generation), H. Virginia (tenth generation), and Helen Belle (Gooch) Twombly (ninth generation).

served as the inn, would not make it through King Philip's wars, the Indian wars that ravaged the countryside. After the family, who all seemed to make it through alive, packed what they could carry and fled for a garrison in Wells, the Indians came through and burned the inn to the ground. But someone had to run the ferry, and a few years later Jedidiah Gooch came back and rebuilt the homestead, also adding a busy tavern. They tavern had a dirt floor until well into the early 1800s and did a fair business selling ale to fishermen and sailors.

Coming Home

Today, the Seaside is a sprawling series of cottages, which are really small homes, and a two-level motel with two rows of rooms, upper and lower, that face the Atlantic. Their enormous grounds include an expanse of lawn dotted with Adirondack chairs, a hammock, an arbor, flowerbeds, and white iron tables and chairs for picnics. In the early 1920s, when my family vacationed across the street at the Forest Hill House, the Seaside had built a fine restaurant; my cousin recalls eating there with the family many times during the 1950s. While they still serve a mean continental breakfast each morning with homemade muffins and fresh-squeezed orange juice, they are out of the food business now.

When I first enter the Seaside's narrow, rounded driveway, I feel like I still have the sense of coming home—even though it's not to our house or the hotel my family stayed in years ago. I would like to say that New York City falls away as soon as I walk through the Seaside's screen door, but it takes a while.

Trish and Ken work the Seaside as hard as her parents did. They have recently vented the place for air conditioning—the biggest technological advance since indoor plumbing. Change comes slowly to the Seaside—I love that. Trish's great-grandmother didn't want indoor plumbing when it became popular. Apparently, she thought it was disgusting and unsanitary to have *that* going on inside one's house!

They have assembled a terrific group of people to work there. Mona McLean makes the muffins most mornings while daughters April and Nancy keep the rooms immaculate. Mona comes from sturdy Down East fishing stock, and when her mother chopped through her finger while chopping up lobsters, she asked Mona to hold the thumb up for her so she could catch the tendons and sew it back on.

⎯⎯⎯⎯⎯∾∾⎯⎯⎯⎯⎯

Today Kennebunkport looks much the same as it did when my grandparents first visited. A little bridge spans the river and people sit at the edge eating fried clams from the Clam Shack, formerly the famous Shackford and Gooch. Dock Square's buildings in Lower Village still stand, though replaced by new stores every generation or so. The theater is gone, as are the candy store and soda fountain; in their place are stores selling beach glass jewelry and Beanie Babies. The square itself has changed little, in summer planted with rows of bright flowers, in winter decorated with a Christmas tree. People are friendly and helpful, still careful to mind their own business but happy to welcome strangers. Store owners remember customers from year to year and the town closes down early, except for the little convenience store, which stays open until 11:00 P.M. in summer.

Usually after a few days of walking around town, going to the flea markets in Wells and Arundel, and eating, I become human again. I eat lobsters, steamers, and all sorts of seafood, reminding me of happy memories from my childhood, my mother's childhood, and even my grandmother's youth. But I can't eat seafood at home—not at my restaurant, anyway. Cooking it for hundreds of people a day over five, six years takes the fun out of it. But as soon as I get to Kennebunkport I happily dive into the first bucket of steamers I can get my hands on. When I walk the beach at low tide and the quahogs are exposed, I long to have a kitchen again so that I can make clam chowder right then. I go to Nunan's Lobster Hut, braving a mosquito onslaught while I wait on line like my customers are forced to wait at Pearl, just to have a lobster served on a tin tray the size of a pizza pan. The pickle chips are out of a tub and the rolls are cafeteria rolls but the lobsters—2 to $1^1/4$ pounders—are amazing, fresh from the sea that afternoon. I log a lot of hours at lobster huts and pounds, like Barnacle Billy's in the Ogunquit space that long ago held the Whistling Oyster Tearoom, getting my fill of chowders and oysters. This is comfort food, reminding me of where I am and where I have been.

But more than anything, it is Kennebunk Beach that makes me feel like I am home again. The cottages, St. Ann's, the old hotels, and the beach house are all relatively unchanged. They look as they've always looked, the way they'll probably always look. I may make my rounds of the other beaches, but I always come back to Gooch's. Walking toward the beach, the grass becomes increasingly sparse until it disappears into the sand. Tiny guests, their heads bobbing up and down like buoys on the water, run through the tall green stalks, knocking beach plums off their branches, while their laughter rises on the wind.

My mother ran through those same grasses, so did I, and so did my nieces, Becca and Sarah, and my nephew, Daniel. After my mom sold the house on Summer Street, I was afraid I wouldn't feel that sense of continuity and family again. I loved that house—it was Maine to me. But over the last two years I have learned something very important. Home for us is not the house that we owned or the one that I eventually hope to buy; it's the whole of the Kennebunks, the beach, the salt marshes, and everything we have come to love about the area—even Pearl. Most of all, Maine will always be home because of our memories.

ACKNOWLEDGEMENTS

Local museums and historical societies are inspiring places filled with dedicated people. Please remember to support their efforts. We are indebted to the following people: Liz Magnuson at the Brickstore Museum in Kennebunk, Maine, volunteers at the Kennebunkport Historical Society; the eminent historian Joyce Butler of the Maine Historical Society; the staffs of the Kennebunk Free Library and the Graves Library in Kennebunkport.

Personal stories give history its mettle and resonance and we thank Margery Orem, who shared her family's history with us. Barbara Collier, a docent at the historic Nott House in Kennebunkport, filled in many gaps in our story and put us in touch with Wallace Reid, bearer of more valuable information.

Dorothy Parsons Christopher was incredibly generous with her personal recollections, which brought many of our stories to life. We cannot thank her enough. Sally J. Barnum, of the Jewish Federation/Jewish United Fund, relentlessly tracked down members of the Goldsmith family, including Rebecca's cousins, Louise and Erika Rosenbaum. Without Louise's terrific memory, this book would have been much the poorer.

The Severance-Mason family at the Seaside Motor Lodge spent many hours discussing Seaside history and always provides unparalleled hospitality. We also thank Mona McLean and daughters April and Nancy for their stories.

Many people helped test the recipes, including friend and chef Cindy Walt, sous chef Edward McFarland, and "tester" Francine Fielding. Evalin Sterns, caterer extraordinaire, was of great help on the photo shoot, where Michael Donnelly took some gorgeous pictures for us. Thanks to Lynn Chase at Riverbank Antiques for the wonderful hotel silver.

ReganBooks and HarperCollins gave us wonderful people to work with, and continued thanks to our publisher, Judith Regan. With love and thanks to agent and friend Claudia Cross of Sterling Lord Literistic.

Deborah thanks Beverly DiClementi, my darling, talented mom, also hailed from a rustic little resort town, Alexandria Bay in upstate New York. A childhood of summers spent on the pink granite shores of the St. Lawrence River proved invaluable to this project, helping me understand the cadence that all small- town resorts share. If only she were here now. My wonderful dad, Frank DiClementi, has supported everything I've ever tried, from my first lemonade stand to this book. It has made the difference.

Rebecca thanks the staff of Pearl Oyster Bar for holding down the fort. My sous chef Edward McFarland, a fisherman at heart and fellow Mainiac, has the difficult job of being me when I'm not there. Without him, I would not have a life. The talented Maria Nazzoli drew the wonderful oysters, lobsters, and food for this book and is also the anchor of our floor staff.

I'd like to thank my brother, David Charles, for the shared memories of our childhood. My mom, Eleanor Goldsmith Charles, has been my role model, my mentor, my adversary, my teacher, and my friend. A "thank you" is woefully inadequate here, but those are the only words I have to express my gratitude.

And finally, to the entire Goldsmith clan, wherever they are, I hope they are pleased with the way we told their story.

Index